Smart People
Smart Business

Smart Business Builders

Dear fellow small business owner,

Welcome to **SMART Business Builders** the first volume of **SMART People SMART Business.**

The idea behind SMART People SMART Business came from one of those fabulous coffee meetings that every small business owner needs to make sure they include in their agenda on a regular basis.

If you don't have a group of colleagues that you meet with regularly, either one on one or in a mastermind group to share ideas, give each other feedback and provide support and encouragement, then I strongly recommend that you do so.

Anyway Fred and I were chatting about what we had been up to in the time since we'd last got together, the challenges we'd faced and overcome (or were still struggling with), the projects we were working on, and of course our achievements.

Fred proudly held up his latest achievement
"An Introduction to Internet Marketing: How to get started in internet marketing" (Volume 1) by Fred Gillen. Fred was a published author. **WOW!!!**

Well of course I was very impressed and thrilled for Fred. But it was when he started to tell me how he had gone about getting published that an opportunity popped into my head and I started to get really excited.

One of the key strategies I recommend for small business owners wanting to build their brand and credibility is to have a book published.... and from what Fred was telling me I suddenly saw an amazing opportunity for small business owners to become published authors on a shoestring budget and in a minimal amount of time by working together to create a shared book. And let's face it money and time are frequently in short supply for small business owners.

Thus the SMART People SMART Business series was born.

Fred and I want to thank the 12 fabulous and VERY SMART business owners who saw the vision and responded to our call for contributors for this first volume, SMART Business Builders. They all produced their chapters in just over a week. An amazing achievement.

We also want to thank Tania and Scott Smith from Typengraphics for the fantastic book cover design.

Also thanks to my partner Colin "The Networking World Cool Tools Geek" who generously gave his time to help with the proof reading. Definitely NOT one of my skills.

Most importantly, from me personally, a HUGE thanks to Fred for sharing the secrets behind getting published with me so that we could open this opportunity for more small business owners to become published authors.

We really hope you enjoy the stories in SMART Business Builders and that the insights, challenges and successes shared by the contributors inspire you to continue on your business journey.

If you would like to be a contributor to a future edition or even publish a book of your own you can find out more at the back of this book.

Best wishes

Brenda Thomson

Contents:

Chapter 1 - An Improbable Business Owner
By: Brenda Thomson

Looking back I am probably not the most likely person to start a business. All the expectations and beliefs that I held as a girl growing up were around; get a good education, go to university, get a profession, start a career before becoming a good wife and mother, being an active member of the community and supporting your husband.

I was born in the Isle of Man. My father was a farmer, a Methodist Minister and a Member of the House of Keys (The Manx Parliament).

I was essentially an only child. My father was 30 years older than my mother. He had a daughter from a first marriage who was already married with family of her own and had immigrated to Australia before I was born. She was the same age as my mother and her children were both older than me.

My Mum had been a nurse who gave up her career to become "John's wife".
But looking back she was so much more than that. She was a leading member of the local community. She too became a Methodist minister; she also took on the role of local Sunday School Teacher and became an active member of the Women's Institute (The equivalent of the Country Women's Association). She also became fascinated with livestock management, planning a cattle breeding program and organising for my father to enter cattle shows. As a result my father became renowned for his prize winning Welsh Black Cattle. In the light of what I know now it was probably her entrepreneurial spirit that was instrumental in turning a subsistence farm into a successful business,, but I am sure my mother would never have seen herself in that light.

I was 8 when my father, then almost seventy, decided it was time to retire and move near his other daughter. So my parents sold the family farm and we moved to Perth, Western Australia.

When we arrived in Australia, determined to give me the best possible start to my education, and against my father's wishes, my mother updated her nursing qualifications and went back to work so that I could go to a private school. So off I went to Methodist Ladies College.

MLC was definitely a good match for the dreams and expectations my mother had for me (although not such a good match for me as a person but that's another story).

I remember in grade 6 the teacher asking all the girls in the class what they wanted to do when they grew up; I was in the 'A' stream, the class for all the "brainy" kids back in the days when classes were streamed on academic ability. I remember it seemed as though half the class said either doctor or lawyer (I was one of the Doctor group), then there was an assortment of scientists and teachers even an opera singer. I don't think anyone said anything to do with business, at least not that I recognised.

What happened to the grade six dream of being a doctor? That fell by the wayside by about year nine when I discovered that I was simply hopeless at the essential subjects of physics, chemistry, geometry and trigonometry. Hopeless, or just not willing to work hard enough? Mmmm..

But by then I had discovered what I was good at; with a lead role in the school play every year from grade 6 to year 12, acting was the obvious choice and my next career ambition was born.. So I finished year 12 with marks just good enough to get me into the course of my dreams (after all why work harder than you need to?)

Fresh out of high school I started a Theatre Arts degree at the West Australian Institute of Technology (what is now WAAPA).

I was there in the same year as Judy Davis. She got the parts I wanted. Suddenly I wasn't the best any more, being an understudy is never much fun and as you may have guessed.. I wasn't the kind of person to fight for what I wanted so I moved the goal posts again.

At about that time I met "the man of my dreams" who was saving to head off on the "Everybody did it in the seventies" backpacker year. Of course that instantly became what I wanted to do too and I threw in uni for a "gap" year.

Then followed 9 months of the traditional "saving to travel" bar-maiding and nannying jobs. I either quit or got fired from all of them but managed to save enough money to head off with my boyfriend backpacking round Europe.

When I got back from overseas I had another brief shot at uni with absolutely no idea about what I wanted to do but still with the ingrained family expectation that you had to have a uni degree and a profession to succeed.

Economics was NOT a good choice. Looking back I have absolutely no idea why I chose it and I am not sure I knew then. I lasted less than three months. So, madly in love... engaged to be married.. and wanting to save up so we could buy a house, I started my first "real" job as a Commonwealth public servant.

My Public Service Career started as a payroll clerk with the Department of Defence, definitely not the job of my dreams and I was nearly ready to quit again. Do you see a pattern happening here?

Then fortunately someone spotted my acting skills and equated my ability to perform on a stage with the ability to stand up in front of a classroom. I got sent off on a "Train the Trainer" course and given a training job.

I spent the next 15 years building a career I loved. In the meantime: getting married, adopting my gorgeous daughter Beth, going through a marriage breakup, being a single mum, going back to uni and getting that oh so important degree (this time it was a Psychology degree and I finished it!!!), remarrying, having a baby, and getting a second qualification, this time a Graduate Diploma in Training and development. All the while steadily getting promoted, including a stint as the Head of Security Audit and Fraud for the Treasury in Canberra. I received several awards for outstanding contributions to the Tax Office and a reputation for being one of the department's top trainers. My Public Service career culminated in a move to Melbourne (with husband Colin, 9 year old Beth and 4 year old Rory in tow) as the Human Resources Advisor for the Tax Office in Box Hill.

Career Changes
I had it all. A wonderful husband, two gorgeous kids, a career I loved, the all important uni degree, a steady income, decent hours, regular holidays. So why on earth did I give all that up to start a business?

Two things happened at about the same time that all came together to change my life forever.. Either one of them alone probably would not have done it.

First, my husband Colin got a permanent job. He had always been a contractor. Working in computers and IT, this was very well paid but not exactly oozing security, and security is something that is ingrained in my value system. Remember, go to uni, get a profession, build a safe career. And I had done exactly that. Back then you didn't get much safer than the public service. But with Colin in a

8

"real" job I didn't need to be the one with the safe secure career any more, I had choices.

Second, our gorgeous, bright, outgoing and intelligent son Rory got to the end of his first year of school unable to even read his name. After visits to paediatricians, audiologists, behavioural optometrists and psychologists and too many tests to count, we were given a diagnosis of "a gifted child with a learning disability". Confronting enough in itself, but made worse by the fact that nobody seemed to have any idea what to do about it.

So faced with a burning desire to do something to help my "baby" and with the security net of a husband with a "safe" job, I threw in the career, cashed in the superannuation and headed off to learn everything I could about reading disabilities including going back to uni to do an honours year followed by three years working on a PhD in reading disabilities.

The years that followed were challenging, exciting and extremely rewarding.

I had several papers published including a presentation at an International Dyslexia Association Special Conference.

Rory learned to read and, based on what I had learned in my research, I started providing private tutoring classes for children with reading disabilities with some great results.

Then disaster struck.. Or at least it looked like it was about to strike. Colin's employer was laying off staff and it looked like he would be next. We had a big mortgage, two children in private schools and of course the lifestyle to match. PhD students don't make much money and my private tutoring clients were limited by the number of hours that I could teach. All my students were one on one and had to be fitted in between 3pm and 6pm on school days or on Saturdays. I had really just created my own job where I was the boss and the employee. I didn't really think of it as a business and I certainly never thought of changing the business model.

So with Colin hanging onto his "safe secure" job by his finger nails we took the plunge and invested our life savings into a web design franchise business. The plan was that Colin would keep working for as long as his job lasted while taking care of the web design part of the business on evenings and weekends. And I would fit building the business, marketing and sales, around my teaching and my research.

According to the plan we would at least be on our way to having a successful business when the axe finally fell on Colin's job. But we knew absolutely NOTHING about starting or running a business, even with the safety net of a franchise, and things do not always go according to plan..

The Networking World story
To put it bluntly the web design business was an expensive disaster, leaving us hundreds of thousands of dollars in debt.

But there was a positive outcome.

I had been told by my franchise trainer that the best way to build our web design business was by networking. In particular she had told me to join a BNI (Business Networking International) chapter and in my search for a BNI Chapter to join I found literally hundreds of other networking groups and opportunities. Some of them were affordable, some expensive, some a total waste of time, others more useful.

The thing that stood out for me was how hard it was to sort the wheat from the chaff and find the right networking opportunities without wasting hundreds of hours and thousand of dollars. Even within the BNI model, assuming it was the right model for you, (and don't get me wrong I think BNI is an awesome network but it isn't for everyone) you might be lucky or you might not, with finding a chapter that was a good fit for your business or your personality.

It was kind of a "Catch 22". Until you have a network, how do you find one? And I saw an opportunity. We had a web design business so we had the technology. I decided to create an online directory of networking groups for small business owners. A one stop shop for networking resources to connect small business owners with the full range of business networking opportunities.

Thus Networking World was born.

And the business has moved from strength to strength. Less than two years later the web design franchise was gone completely and Networking World was a full time business employing not just me but also my daughter Beth who had finished school and university.

While we started as a Directory of Networking Groups, we rapidly expanded to include a calendar of networking events, networking training courses and finally an online network to connect business owners together to help and support one another.

I had developed, almost by accident, a unique approach to networking. Based on the concept of small business owners working together to create WIN WIN alliances, joint ventures, support networks and mastermind groups. Together Everyone Achieves More!

The Networking World approach was driven by what I had found to work for me, my personality and my value system; by what I saw working for successful business owners and last but definitely not least, by what my clients told me they wanted.

And the fantastic thing about it was… you didn't need to be a social butterfly, have a great sixty second infomercial or be able to work a room to make it work for you. All you needed was a clear business vision and a genuine commitment to working with other people so everyone WINS!

Three years later Colin has joined me in the business as our technology director (The Cool Tools Geek). This has given us the ability to further develop our website. Networking World now holds a unique place in the Australian market as a Network of Networks connecting small business owners not just to a range of networking opportunities but also creating direct connections between business owners across networking groups to create strategic alliances, joint ventures, referral groups, power teams, mastermind groups and support networks. It's all about connecting like minded business owners who genuinely care about helping and supporting each other and creating WIN WIN outcomes for everyone.

We have even moved into running networking groups based on a model developed from over five years of research and experience of what small business owners are looking for in networking opportunities. These SMART Networking Forums are another new step in the evolution of the business.

What have been the challenges issues and learnings?
I know for a fact that the biggest obstacle in my business has been me!

Remember the school girl who quit whenever the going got a bit tough? And the woman for whom a safe secure job was all important? Well they're both still there and I have to keep a very careful eye that they don't get a say in the decision making. Sometimes a nice safe secure job looks soooo inviting!

12

Then there is my love of creating something new. Sometimes I think we have had some incredibly confused clients as I have come up with yet another new idea, a new membership program or a new training course.

Another huge challenge for me has been learning to ask for, receive and act on feedback (particularly when it wasn't at all what I wanted to hear!). But I am so glad I have because it has been a huge factor in the success of Networking World.

What have been the highlights and successes?

Home Based Business of the Year Award
Winning the Home Based Business of the Year Award in 2008 was an amazing turning point for Networking World and for me personally. After three years of struggling, wondering if I was doing the right thing, changing the business model over and over again. It made all the difference to have that level of affirmation that we were providing a valuable service and that we had an award worthy business. Plus being able to use that in my marketing and promotion has been HUGE!

The first 10K month
Winning the Home Based Business of the Year Award was a fantastic achievement but if the amount of money the business was making at that time had been part of the criteria for success I can tell you right here and now, I couldn't have won.
It was initially an incredible struggle to work out a financially viable business model for Networking World. Nobody else was doing what I was doing. While people raved about the wonderful services we offered they were often not prepare to pay for it. It's taken a while but having finally found a business model that works, our first ten thousand dollar month has to be one of the highlights of the business journey.

Being referred to as a mentor and as an inspiration.
Wow! It is the most incredible feeling when successful business people that you know, like and respect, refer to you as an inspiration and as someone they look up to as a mentor and advisor. You know who you are.. Thankyou!

Having created something that really adds value
But by far the biggest highlight so far is the satisfaction of having kept on going through the tough years to create something unique that genuinely adds value to the lives and businesses of Australian small business owners.

6 Top Tips

1. Have a plan
The times when I have been successful have been when I have been working strictly to plan. When I forget to look at the plan, even if only for a month or two, things start to slip. That doesn't mean that the plan has to be set in concrete. To the contrary, be prepared to review, revise and reinvent your plan on a daily and weekly basis, but always have and follow a plan.

2. Get a TEAM
I'm not talking about a team of staff (that depends on your business). One of the key things I have learned over the past five years is that successful business owners don't try to go it alone. It has been my incredible team of alliance partners, mentors, fellow master-minders, advisors, and colleagues, who have enabled me to build Networking World to where it is today.

3. Manage the money
Learn about the finances in your business. Set financial goals, set a budget, know your numbers. A business has the most incredible ability to consume money and not make any if you let it. I had a coach that I couldn't afford for a while. What he taught me about understanding the

finances in the business meant that I fired him. But he was worth every cent he cost me!

4. Learn, learn, learn (but DON'T use not knowing as an excuse for not doing)

In business (and in life) there will always be a million things you don't know. Keep on learning but don't let NOT knowing stop you from acting. If you wait until you know it all before you act.. you will never act. I can't begin to count the thousands of dollars I have spent on training and personal development. I don't regret a cent of it. What I do regret are all the times I didn't take action because I was still afraid of what I didn't know.

5. Listen to your customers

No matter how good your idea is, it's only a good idea if it's what people want and are prepared to pay for. Constantly ask and listen to the responses.

Before we first started Networking World I asked every business owner in my network whether they thought it was a good idea or not. With a resounding 80% plus saying they thought it was, we decided to go ahead. (In retrospect it might have been a good idea to listen a little earlier to the ones who asked.. "How are you going to make it pay?" Fortunately now water under the bridge.)

Since then we have regularly surveyed our clients and newsletter subscribers at least once a year and we are constantly changing and tweaking what we offer based on those responses.

6. Enter Awards

Don't be afraid to enter awards. Entering the "Home Based Business of the Year" award in 2008 was the second most significant marketing factor in my business next to strategic alliances. Even if you don't win you'll learn and grow from the experience. Many awards provide some sort of report on your business, but even if they don't, the process of entering still makes you focus on what you are doing well and where there is room for improvement.

Where to now for Networking World?
I am incredibly excited about the future for Networking World.

What started out as a simple on line directory listing over 1,400 networking groups, has grown into a nationally recognised networking training organisation and an incredible network of fabulous business owners who are genuinely committed to working together and helping and supporting one another.

Many of them have become my good friends as well as business colleagues and clients. Working together we are achieving some amazing results with more and more opportunities developing as the network grows.

If you are an Australian Small Business owner and you're passionate about growing your business but you don't want to go it alone and you'd like to be part of a team of business owners who genuinely care about helping each other achieve great results; or if you run a networking group and you want to be part of a network of networks where everybody works together so we all win, then I'd love you to join us.

How to contact me
If you would like to contact me at anytime, you can visit my website, or eMail me at:
  brenda@networkingworld.net.au

And remember *Network SMARTer Not Harder*

Written by: Brenda Thomson
www.networkingworld.net.au

Chapter 2 - Time Well Spent
By: Karen Glass

The Beginning!
It was "fait accompli"! My dream to start my own business. I believe it all started when I was 15, the official age you could start work in Melbourne, Australia - a young girl with aspirations to achieve. I was independent, hungry to work hard and with a family trait of wanting to please people. I started to yearn for success at an early age.

I started with part time jobs throughout my studies of Diploma of Teaching (Early Childhood). After completing this I proceeded to work in Kindergartens and Managing Child Care Centres for 9 years. It was during this time that the seeds were being planted, and I got the sense that I would like to run my own business. There seemed to be pros and cons as I delved into many small business opportunities to determine where I was best placed to utilise my skills.

I possessed this tough hard work ethic that I felt was better placed in business rather than teaching, although many of the teaching skills were leverageable.

I started reading business books to gain insights on other people's journeys and realised that I had a lot of learning to do. What has inspired me the most is The E Myth Revisited by Michael E Gerber. He says "At its best, your business is something apart from you, rather than a part of you, with its own rules and its own purposes."

Once you recognise that the purpose of your life is not to serve your business, but that the primary purpose of your business is to serve your life, you can then go to work ON your business, rather than IN it, with a full understanding of why it is absolutely necessary for you to do so."

I enrolled in a Certificate IV in Small Business and set about learning the structures, culture, management and financial aspects of businesses. I used this knowledge to work in office management when I moved to the UK in 2000 with my husband for a travel and working holiday.

During our stay there we enjoyed many journeys to European countries that inspired us with architectural brilliance and wonderful wines and breathtaking landscapes. At this time I worked in Office and Project Management, employed within the University of London, where one of the key tasks was managing people as well as their time and projects... I also had the yearning for more knowledge and completed a Certificate in Human Resource Practice whilst living in London, hoping to learn more about people and recruitment within business.

Since returning from London in 2003, I have completed a Certificate IV in Business Administration and various short courses to continually gather new skills.

I had been contemplating starting a family but also possessed a strong desire to work for myself. I am unsure why this festered inside me... perhaps the satisfaction of being successful in my own right and mind or maybe the chance to extend my knowledge and skills through learning new roles and studies.

Motivating reasons
In 2004 we were blessed with a gorgeous daughter who delighted our days with bright blue eyes and a very placid nature. Any spare time I had was spent on the internet searching for that business opportunity that might come along my way. I returned to part time work after a year at home, as a purchasing officer, but sensed deep down that this was just an interim role until I could hit upon something more stimulating.

Then in 2007 we had our second child a little boy who was also such a delightful and easy going child. After this crucial time spent at home with them, I soon realised that the next job that I tackled was going to be one where I could operate from home, obtain a work/life balance and be able to function around my young family. These were my key driving factors into finding a role that gave me this flexibility.

I needed variable work hours so that I would still be able to go along to music and sport with them and witness them enjoy, learn and grow through the younger years, as we all know children grow up way too quickly and I didn't want to miss this important phase in their life.

In 2008 I discovered virtual administration and immediately realised this was the perfect role for me. Many times I have been asked to define Virtual Administration- although it has existed for some time it is still a relative new working methodology for small to medium businesses.

A virtual business owner will work with businesses according to their skill set. For example my skills are in personal, organisational, administration and recruitment so I work alongside clients who need personal assistance, event organisation and management, recruitment administration and general client or customer service (database management). Other virtual services may offer transcription, proofreading or graphic design services and I believe it is important to work within your own skills so that you can provide the highest quality service to your clients.

As virtual administration is a fairly new phenomenon in Australia (it has been widely recognised more so in the past few years) when businesses were looking for ways to optimise administration costs and/or avoid employing new full time staff members.

The benefits being: no PAYG taxes, no annual, long service or sick leave and the opportunity to outsource some of the administrative tasks that took them away from growth and business development within their businesses. Another benefit is that for an employer they can choose the amount of hours that we work therefore not paying staff for quieter periods throughout the year.

Virtual administration has been developed to assist women and men (yes there are men in this industry too!) to go back into the workforce with the flexibility and options to work the hours that suits their particular circumstances.

From research it seemed virtual administration required the key skills of exceptional time and organisational management and this was my forte. I delved into the industry a little more and realised there were many similar people looking to operate from home to find that happy medium of an acceptable work/life balance. Consequently my VA journey emanated from this assessment.

I eased into creating the business, by becoming a Member of ACS (A Claytons Secretary) and this provided me with the opportunities to learn from others online. There was such a wonderful online support forum from other members to give advice, ask questions and provide assistance when needed It also provided job leads and I was able to start working with Dragon Personnel as a Recruitment Administrator in the first month of commencing my business.

In the first year I hastened slowly and developed my business name "Time Well Spent". The business name came from considering what type of service I was going to offer the clients and what benefits they were going to receive. Simple but effective logic. Basically working with a virtual administrator ensures each client uses our services to the benefits of their business so their time is well spent.

I started with setting up the business by writing a business plan that included both business and personal goals. Writing a business plan with short term and long term goals gave me clarity about where I wanted to take the business and how I was going to do it. It has been beneficial to review the document every quarter to reassess the business plan and also gain a real sense of achievement as some of the short term goals were realised.

I undertook to ascertain all the intricacies for developing my own website and set about learning as much as possible about software and web based programs that would add value to my current knowledge and abilities. Running your own business also meant being your own time, IT and organisational Manager - there was no one else there dictating stringent timetables and unmanageable deadlines, so it was important to stay focussed.

I had the expectation that working as a virtual administrator would provide one off services for clients for ad hoc tasks or projects, but oddly enough this was not the case. Most of my clients currently have been with me for over a year, some for 2.5 years and I believe this has come from loyalty, honesty and working together effectively to grow their businesses.

For business sustainability it was imperative that it centred on getting the balance right between working ON the business and IN the business. This balance had to be structured managing all the clients and tasks in the most efficient way possible. I embraced the new knowledge I was acquiring from forums and membership of networking groups and used this proficiency to develop long term business relationships with some wonderful colleagues.

How to get out there!
In a virtual environment there needs to be some innovative

ways to market your business so that people know of your existence. The best form of advertising was by word of mouth so I joined networking groups and attended events where I could liaise and interact with people and listen to their experiences. This was a really important point of difference, which my services could offer to their business. "By seeking to understand you can then be understood" was my mantra.

I also made a decision to participate in online forums and blogs and set my website up as an information portal, so that potential clients could recognise the valuable services and insights that Time Well Spent could provide to help grow their business. At this point money spent on marketing and advertising was negligible, as word of mouth and networking events have been effective marketing tools.

All businesses need to have a point of difference and although I am "virtual" I still attend events for my clients, business meetings, launches, training seminars etc. This is something that not every virtual administrator can provide, due to their location, service offering or personal circumstances.

I decided that I would like to continue my professional development through joining Women's Network Australia and The Bayside Business Network in 2009 as well as many online forums that provided means and ways of learning and meeting new people.

I commenced working with clients on many different projects, from administration of a networking group, customer service follow up calls, internet research and recruitment administration. Initially I was uncertain of my final aim and what and where my proficiencies and capabilities would lead me, so I ventured into many subsidiary areas – trial and error on many occasions.

Eventually I collaborated with various companies to develop and expand their business growth and this lead onto marketing strategies, marketing plans, publishing books and generating new marketing initiatives. This new area of expertise has been a wonderful addition to the business and one that I am continually expanding each day.

Interestingly when I embarked on this business, I thought that the majority of my clients would be small to medium business owners and this has turned out to be true.

Job opportunities continued to come my way and by January of 2009 I was forced to make the decision to quit my part time role and concentrate fully on my business. From then on I have never looked back.

After nearly 3 years in the business though, I have become more selective about the type of work that I take on as I have now developed skills in a few particular areas that I would really like to expand upon and develop further.

One of those areas is working with Consultants who are also working for themselves. They were seeking executive personal management of projects, diary and travel organisation in addition to marketing and overall management of the day to day happenings in the business. This type and style of work is what I really enjoy, it suited and stimulated me mentally and I have found it to be both very rewarding and satisfying.

The business has grown throughout the past 2.5 years and it has been an amazing journey of self discovery. I have learned so much more about myself... my weaknesses (never being able to say no to extra work), crossing the boundaries many times of work/life balance, burning the candle at both ends, and also taking on too much at any one time.

I have also learnt a lot about my strengths and these are definitely highly effective communication skills with extremely efficient organisational and time management skills which pave the way for growth. In addition my own self-esteem has risen to a noticeable level. Stephen R Covey who wrote "The 7 Habits of Highly Effective People" states that "the first and most basic habit of a highly effective person in any environment, is the *habit of proactivity*" This means that it is more than just merely taking initiative - we have to take our own initiative and personal responsibility to make it happen.

This is crucial in my business especially in client meetings where we are discussing new marketing or business strategies. In offering ideas and services that the client could use I often refer other businesses that could assist them if I am not the right person for the role. (For example, website design, graphic design, etc)

As a business starts to grow, so do issues with regard to time and ability to service each client's needs. Having experienced such growth I needed to work on a structure of outsourcing some of the time consuming tasks. This was a valuable experience in regard to my personal values and commitment to the quality of work provided to the client. The main issue was that I needed to continually coach and mentor these people to achieve the same quality outputs. This outsourcing of work created a different kind of stress. Inefficiency in the use of time and personal resource meant a new set of processes/controls were to be implemented.

I now have developed templates, with guidelines, time boundaries and provided specific instructions which have helped immensely in providing an outcome that is acceptable to the high standards I hold for myself and my clients I have also documented processes and procedures in the form of an Operation Manual for each of my clients so that I can effectively train new staff that join the company.

What lies ahead!
In January of 2011 I will be extending the business by adding another person in a full time capacity. This has been the biggest decision I have had to make so far, but it is needed to continue the growth of the business. This person will be trained in all aspects of my business and will be able to assist in maintaining the high quality of work that I expect.

Michael Gerber's earlier advice about how we need to strike the balance of working ON your business rather than always working IN your business is now solidly coming through and I feel that this will be the most important aspect in the years to come.

The most surprising thing that has happened has been the growth in such a quick space of time. The loyalty of my clients has been tremendous and they have kindly passed on my details if they feel that my services would be of value to other clients, as I mentioned earlier the best marketing campaign is by word of mouth.

I have found my niche and how I grow my business is completely up to me. What is of utmost importance is family time and therefore keeping the work/life balance. Growth won't happen for growth's sake, it will be at my discretion.

The possibilities are numerous and endless and the rewards. *"If it is to be it is up to me."*

Bibliography:
Covey R Stephen "The 7 Habits of Highly Effective People" – Simon and Schuster, New York.1996
Gerber E Michael " The E Myth Revisited" – Harper Collins publishing 1995

Written by: *Karen Glass*
www.timewellspent.com.au

Chapter 3 - Superlearner
By: Marilyn Martyn

My childhood was spent in Adelaide South Australia and it was wonderful. Because Adelaide was a small town, it was safe, so I had a lot of freedom.

Dad was a returned soldier from the Second World War, serving as a gunner defending Darwin. Mum was born and bred in Adelaide although she escaped to Melbourne for a short time. She met Dad in Melbourne when she was a WAAF in the Women's Auxiliary Air Force.

Mum reluctantly returned to Adelaide because Dad believed it offered the best career opportunities and lifestyle for their growing family.

Both my parents were creative and adventurous. Dad's post war career in acting and radio announcing ensured I met a number of celebrities. Hopalong Cassidy, a very popular U.S. film cowboy, being one of them.

I was impressed by the arts and acting community and knew many of the radio actors of the time. I was fascinated by radio and even had a starring role in an advertisement when I was eight. I was paid for my services - my first paying job. With it I asked my parents to buy A.A Milne's, The House at Pooh Corner. I still have it!

Dad worked for the ABC and later went into advertising. Mum was the homemaker. She did a fabulous job raising four children. She loved reading and was a great conversationalist. She influenced me greatly in my need to do more than raise a family. I know she felt trapped and unfulfilled. My love of learning is due totally to her influence.

The post war years in Australia were quite austere but I remember them fondly. I attended state primary and secondary schools full of baby boomer children. Classes were up to 50 children.

The curriculum concentrated on the 3Rs. 3Rs is short for **R**eading, w**R**iting and a**R**ithmatic. However my home life made up for school's limitations. Surrounded by books and an avid reader I did well at school and developed a love of learning – not academic but in areas related to people, writing, books and business.

During the sixties we left Adelaide to live in Melbourne. I found the change easy to cope with but went back to visit relatives in Adelaide frequently.

As a career path, I chose teaching because I could always work and still look after the children which I wanted to have. Women were not encouraged to develop a career in those days. Nurses and teachers were the exceptions.

Women's Liberation was just stirring and there was not the career openings for women that there are today.
Always restless and seeking new learning experiences, I graduated as a teacher, then librarian and taught in primary, secondary and independent schools.

I was not a typical government employee. Often feeling stifled by the restrictions of the Education Department, I still found many alternative means of employment within the system. One of my strengths is, if I see an opportunity to try something new, I'll take it.

I married a South Australian whom I met in Melbourne. Like my mother he had escaped Adelaide. We have 2 sons, who are now in their thirties, with children of their own. It is eerie how situations are repeated.

Realising I was restless like my father; I tried a number of avenues all centred around books, schools, learning and writing.

I began my business career as an educational publisher's representative. I visited hundreds of schools selling the books and material published by this company. I found I really enjoyed selling because of all the people I met.

I learnt how to look after my customers and keep in regular contact. The freedom of being on the road was also appealing. However I was desperate to get experience away from education.

One of the three most traumatic experiences I have experienced in my life was when my husband was diagnosed with bowel cancer. Our sons were only seven and eight at the time. My husband's courage during this time was enormous.

Family and friends also supported us. My husband made a full recovery, however we were hit financially. Fortunately I was able to get a job as a publisher's representative. I was out of school at last!

I was responsible for book sales to general bookshops in Victoria and Southern N.S.W. I discovered I really enjoyed building up a client base and reaching my sales targets. It was on a part time basis. I had the school holidays and shorter hours than normal. I also met famous authors. Colleen McCullough is one who stands out. I also met Barry Jones. Part of my job was also to get ideas for books that could be published.

For the next few years I remained in publishing and also tutored students in reading.

The two other traumatic situations followed. Our marriage failed and our youngest son contracted leukaemia soon after. I cannot explain the level of grief I felt on both occasions. My son, like his father, showed the same courage. His elder brother was a perfect match for a bone marrow transplant. My son no longer has cancer.

I knew how lucky I was to have the skills to support myself, and an Education Department that kept welcoming me back. Doors keep opening for me. It was really uncanny. It was as if someone was guiding me. I am not reluctant to admit that I do ask for God's guidance.

Apart from my family, the passion in my life is reading and writing. I think this is why I kept returning to schools. I have to be honest too - it was also secure. Business is far riskier. I remember one of my mentors telling me I might find it impossible to move from the protection of being an employee to one of being an entrepreneur. He left me more than a little shaken at this news.

Reading is one of the most important skills anyone can learn. There is enormous satisfaction seeing a student develop reading and writing skills.

I trained in 'Reading Recovery' and 'Spalding' to make sure I knew what I was doing. They are in depth literacy training courses.

I remember clearly how I learnt to read. I have found all the books in the reading series that was used. The depth of these books is quite amazing. I realised why I am such an advocate of incorporating systematic phonics (learning the relationship between letters and sounds) in teaching someone to read. That is how I was taught.

An internet eBook publishing company has published a book written by me on the subject. I also received payment for the manuscript.

I won an international poetry award. I decided to enter a contest in the US and entered a poem I had written about a young student of mine who had such a wonderful attitude to life. My poem, 'The Student' was a runner up in the contest and was published in a hard bound volume. I dedicated it to my mother. I was invited to Washington to share other poems. This was a problem because I have only written one!

I was also dismayed to learn how many people have no respect for the education system.

There are two sides to every story. Teachers have been expected to take on the roles of parents and have to deal regularly with a significant number of students who do not want to learn (in school!).

Parents need to look at their role in their child's upbringing more closely and support schools more. Parents know how important it is to read to young children on a daily basis, for only a few minutes, but so many say they haven't the time. Panic starts in secondary school when students are hit with the reality that their lack of skills attracts.

Believe me it isn't hard to learn to read as a young child provided the instruction is enlightened. It gets significantly more difficult as one gets older.

My experience in sales and marketing was an eye opener and such fun. I went to sales training and personal development courses.

After attending many business seminars and being inspired by many people who had the courage to start their own business and face up to the inevitable challenges I finally decided to give it ago. Naturally it is around education, teaching and writing.

I am developing my business because of the personal growth it offers and the people I meet. My only regret is I didn't wake up to the opportunity many years ago. But I firmly believe it is never too late. And despite our youth oriented society, I know I still have a lot to give.

During the past decade I trialled software for the Learning Federation in primary and secondary schools and have seen the possibility of developing an online business as well as an offline writing business. Technology will make education more personalised. I am all for it!

I set up a tutoring business. I began as a tutor for the Commonwealth Government's Evenstart Tutoring Program in 2007 and 2008. I established my company, Elimar Products and Services. It offers individual tutoring for children, teenagers and adults. I also gained a support teacher contract. I also sub contract to a tutoring company. I source top educational software to market online.

My website www.superlearner.com.au is designed to market both my services and first rate educational programs. For the first time I have taken responsibility for managing my career. I am proactive. I am surrounding myself with like minded people who are inspiring and keep me on track.

I know if you have a passion for something and are totally committed to reaching your goals, doors open.

Superlearner online began with a blog, phonicsforkids.net This is where I learned to write articles that are keyword optimised. It has been exciting to receive comments from people from numerous countries about the content. However there is a lot to learn about the Internet and it is not as easy to master as I had hoped. Getting keywords right is one of a number of skills still to master - and as for technical aspects!!!!!!!!!!!

I acknowledge how important it is to have a technical expert to support my online activities. I have already met one such person who is also a great marketer.

A successful online business, Superlearner, has been my goal for well over 5 years and it is well on track. The learning curve has been steep. It was when I found people to support me that everything began to fall into place.

People can now log into www.superlearner.com.au and receive online lessons, join webinars or receive individual tuition. I have sourced some educational products to market and I aim for this to expand. I also have time to write which I enjoy no end. At present I am working at expanding this area of the business.

The Internet has, and will continue to revolutionise how people connect, learn and do business. I am excited by the prospect of my business growth.

Over the past three years or so I have been attending seminars run by people who have had great success using the Internet. At first I found what they had to say overwhelming. But I kept plugging away. At the same time I began to receive some writing commissions. The first was from an internet marketer in the US, who asked me to rewrite some copy on a website he was setting up for a client. I then researched some topics for him about local search engine optimisation.

An Australian wholesaler asked me to write about 'The Tree of Life' for a product he was marketing. As a result my second poem was born. I also have a contract for researching and writing five articles a week for an American company that specialises in writing for blogs. I am also writing lessons for my website which also has a blog that needs constant content.

The future looks exciting. I am fascinated by how people tick, so plan to interview as many as I can. I also aim to write content for company blogs here in Melbourne. I have learned a number of lessons regarding business over the past five or so years, but a lot more about life. Life is a wonderful adventure with many challenges along the way.

My business grew when I put my plan in writing. Having a published business plan and goals changed my outlook. As you have probably realised I can be easily distracted by the next colourful object. It was only when I consciously stopped myself from doing this that my business direction became clear.

My next bit of advice is to keep trial and error to a minimum. Seek out and learn from successful people. Most are more than willing to share their expertise. Be willing to admit your mistakes. They are positive. No mistakes - no growth. Above all keep up self-education. It is always beneficial to work more on yourself than your business. It is important to acknowledge you don't know it all and never will. A freeing thought that.

Always be in contact with skilled people who can add to your business.

Be sure to network for friendship, support and inspiration. I am a member of a women's networking group and am constantly inspired by what the members are achieving. I learn more when I am giving.

My last word is - have a dream and believe in it. It doesn't matter how long it takes for it to come true.
I am sure you have heard life is about the journey and not the destination.

I wish you all the success in your life and business.

Written by: *Marilyn Martyn*
www.superlearner.com.au

Chapter 4 - Nitty Gritty Business
By: Fred Gillen

When I first discussed with Brenda (Thomson) the possibility of producing this book it was around the concept of compilations of stories from other small business owners.

I never really thought of including my story until I started to enlighten Brenda as to my past endeavours.

As I started to open up I realised that my story may be of interest after all. Maybe I should have titled this chapter "An Interesting Life".

So let's get into it.

Where it all started:
I immigrated to Australia from Ireland in the early seventies as a newly qualified electrician, so that will give you some idea of my age.

The real interesting part of that major decision was why I actually decided to come here. You see for me at the time the decision was really easy. I had just completed my apprenticeship in Dublin, Ireland and it was time to leave the nest. I was thinking of trying my luck in the UK when I became aware of a special offer being made by the Australian Government. They were looking for trades people, and were prepared to pay the travel costs in return for staying in Oz for 2 years.

The only other commitment on my side was a ten pound good will payment. So the decision was: fly to the UK for twenty seven pounds or fly to Melbourne for ten... as I said.... the decision was easy. **Melbourne here I come!**

The First Few Years

For the first few years I moved from job to job chasing the money, you could do it in those days as work was plentiful and trades people were in high demand.

I then started my own electrical contracting business and quickly realised that you needed to specialise if you were going to develop a viable business, so I concentrated on the Industrial sector and in particular servicing induction molding machines and other electronically controlled machinery.

Because of this my interest in electronics grew and I attended night school and became qualified in Industrial Electronics. This was in the early eighties as the personal computer was starting to come on the scene.

My first PC was a Tandy TRS 80 and because of my new found interest in computers I formed a group of enthusiasts. To cut a long story short we worked together to build interfaces to extend the capabilities of the Tandy, including a device that allowed the electric typewriter of the time (the selectric) to be connected and form a very crude word-processor / printer combination.

The IBM clones became available during this period and I started to import components and sell assembled PC's to friends, family, etc. This led to me establishing a PC retail outlet in Bonbeach, a seaside suburb of Melbourne.

Suddenly I had moved from being a self employed electrical contractor to being a sales person in a retail store and I just loved it. The interaction with the customers was fantastic, sharing the new found knowledge about PC's gave me a real buzz.

The business grew and I engaged 2 part time staff to help manage the work load. This growth period lasted for a number of years but then like everything, things change.

International suppliers set up shop and started to discount and sell direct, this caused a drop in margins and meant that we had to sell more. This in turn caused a reduction in the amount of service we could supply to each retail customer. Customer service is number one in my book and I just could not come to terms with not being in a position to offer the best service at all times.

For me the writing was on the wall and it was time to move. Again I decided to specialise and target a small, unique sector of the market. This time it was small business networks, not business networking as we know it today, but connecting small groups of PC's together in an office environment so that employees could share files.

Again this was new technology that had previously only been available to the big corporates but was now being made available to small business owners. So the services were in high demand and I could charge reasonable fees for my services.

I closed the retail business and moved into the consultancy arena. During the last fifteen years I have consulted to various small businesses, government departments and major insurance companies.

I have been engaged in all areas of IT, from equipment deployment to software development and project management and loved every minute of it.

I have learnt a lot along the way and can certainly say that my people skills have changed for the better. In the early days I was more of an instructor and would tell people what to do, these days I would hope that I am more of a mentor and share my knowledge and draw the best out of people.

That's enough about my history, now to what I'm involved in right now.

Internet Marketing
(Why I love it)

I guess the reason I am now so involved in Internet Marketing is because the playing field is changing every day and you need to be on your toes.

With my love of IT and more recently Business Marketing it was obvious I would be attracted to the Internet.

Over the years I have often be asked for advice by other small business owners on what IT systems they should use within their business and often the conversation would get around to marketing.

So suddenly the light seemed to go on..... These two things were very important to any small business especially to newly established ones.

The other thing that happened which pushed me in this direction occurred at a business networking meeting I attended in Melbourne a couple of years ago. As I was listening to attendees talking about their challenges with marketing using the internet I realised that I had the opportunity to again share my knowledge and enhance my business as well.

Internet marketing is now a must have tool within any business, I guess you could say if you're not found on Google then you're not going to be found. So as part of my consulting services I started to offer training on using the internet to promote business.

The problem was that I now seemed to be offering a lot of services and gave the impression that I was not focused on any particular area. My customers were getting confused.

I would often get asked 'What are you doing today" which kind of suggested that my clients really did not have a clue what I really did. Little had changed, I actually was offering a variety of services, all aligned with IT and marketing, but my clients were still confused.

I was clearly giving out the wrong perception and as the saying goes "Perception Is Reality" so I had to do something.

Time for Branding:
So last year I decided to go through a re-branding exercise and established "The Nitty Gritty Business Group", this now makes it easier for me to explain to both my current and future clients that I have multiple service areas which are all aligned and designed to work together to bring the best outcome for my clients.

The world of business is changing and the world is getting smaller because of the advances in technology. I always have and always will use technology to enhance my business.

For example..... I really now operate in the virtual world. More and more business is done over email and Skype than ever before, I can honestly say that 50% of my day is now spent on the computer communicating with my virtual team.

I now have a team of assistants available from all over the world that work while I sleep, so the works seems to get done faster, things are moving faster than ever before and you need to move with it.

I am becoming more of an organiser and project manager that a doer, although I must admit I still enjoy getting my hands dirty.

I am constantly researching trends from overseas because history shows that the successful ideas implemented overseas will be implemented here shortly after.

As part of my business building plan I also attend business network meetings to establish relationships so that I can spread the word about my services,

Some would say I am a habitual networker, in the current meaning of the word, what I mean by that is that I attend business network meetings whenever I can and as part of that process and by listening to attendees, I fine tune my market strategy to suit the market.

I have learnt over the years that you can no longer rely on old marketing methods. You can't just sit back and expect new clients to just drop in, you now have to be proactive and make it easier for them to find you.

Faxes are being replaced by emails, land lines are being replaced by mobiles.

Years ago the Yellow Pages was how people found you, but that has changed too.

The web is the way of the future and that is why I am riding that train.

Today my main customer research tool is, you guessed it. GOOGLE.....

I can even check up on my competitors and see how their marketing efforts are working and if they know what they are doing they can check on me.

That is why I am now concentrating on assisting other small business owners to use technology to firstly find out where their market is and then help them set up systems to attract those customers searching the Internet for their particular services or products.

Where is all this going, I have no Idea but I know that I will be watching with eyes wide open to make sure I don't get left behind.

As a matter of interest, you can check up on me if you like, just type in *Fred Gillen* in the search box on Google.

Let me know what you find.

Many Strings
As I said before, I now have a variety of services available to my clients and I'll explain why I have decided to go down this path rather that focus on any one area.

About three years ago I came up with a marketing concept that I thought had real merit and I decide to focus solely on that.

I established a business called "Coffee Cup Promotions", the concept was to sell advertising on take-a-way coffee cups.

There was a whole marketing, promotional and distribution plan set in place and we made the cost affordable to the smaller business owner by dividing the take-away-cup into three advertising spaces.

We had distribution arrangements with lots of coffee outlets in the CBD area of Melbourne, one particular outlet moving 4000 cups for us each week.

The problem was that we were totally reliant on the advertising dollar and our clients having funds available for advertising.

Then the bomb hit... the GFC.... everyone ran scared and the first thing they cut was the advertising spend. We where out of business overnight, I attempted to ride it out for a while but time was not on my side so I bit the bullet and moved on.

The lesson I learnt from this, let's call it a business adventure, was that you cannot control your market, you can only supply it if it's there.

This adventure made that easier to understand and I quickly learnt "Don't put all your eggs in one basket".

That is why now I effectively have a tool box with lots of tools available to help my clients, it just depends which one is needed at the time.

I no longer put all my eggs in one basket.

I'll give you an idea of how I have achieved this. It is all driven by my clients needs.

Let's take our Newsletter Creation service "Nitty Gritty Newsletters". This all stemmed from one of our existing clients having the need to stay in contact with a group that attended classes at their store.

They had no idea how to do it and had no inclination to find out. I suggested they outsource it but we could not locate anyone to do it, so we created the service in house and now offer it to other clients as well.

The other side of the coin came from the businesses that did want to do it themselves but did not know where to start. I trained them in the process as part of my consulting service and at the same time created a home study / DIY pack which we now offer on-line.

And the final example I'll give here is a further extension of this training. In October 2010 we ran our 1st live Hands-On workshop that gave attendees the knowledge to create and maintain their own web presence.

All of these offerings are unique in their own right but have a common thread of assisting small business to grow.

It also means that if one area goes a bit slow then maybe the other will cover some of the downturn.

I have seen a lot of businesses fail due to the fact they rely on one particular product or service and the market disappears. There was nothing wrong with what they had on offer it was just that the market no longer required it.

That is why my business is constantly changing, I try and listen to what the market wants and then see if there is a way I can supply it.

As this book will demonstrate, both Brenda and I believe that there is a market for this type of product, we pooled our resources and brought it to market.

The fact you are reading it now shows us that it was a good idea.

My business today is not the same as it was last year and I can guarantee you that it won't be the same next year.

Will all of the services I offer now still be available?
Probably not.

Will I have additional services available to assist my clients?
You can bet on it.

The one thing I have learnt over my thirty plus years in business is that you have to be prepared for change and grab it with both hands, if you don't then your competition probably will and you will get left behind.

I never say no to a new idea, my answer always is *"Let Me Think About It"* how long or how hard I think about it depends on the idea.

I guess if anyone asked me what I focus on I'd have to answer *"I focus on change"*, I attempt to watch the market, anticipate change and see if I can at least be part of it or pre-empt it.

The particular market I operate in is changing every day so I am kept pretty busy.

As a final note there is one other thing that I'd like to mention and that is I am seriously working on building my team of virtual assistants, and the primary reason for that is to allow me to take time out of the business.

As a small or solo business owner it is very hard to take time out because when you are not there, there is no income coming in or being created.

As my team become more involved I will be able to reduce my involvement in the day to day operations and concentrate on developing new business opportunities.

That means that the business itself should be in a position to run without me for at least a couple of weeks per year.

It also means that I am developing a sale-able asset, a business that is not totally reliant on one person's expertise.

This is probably something you should think about too, but I'm not here to preach.

I hope you have enjoyed reading about my history and business adventures.

It actually brought back some good and bad memories as I put these words on paper.

But there is only one thing we can do (or should do) with the past and that is .... **learn from it.**

How to contact me
If you would like to contact me at anytime with a business related question or idea, you can visit my website, or email me at: fred@fredgillen.com

Till next time we meet.....

Have a fantastic time

Written by: *Fred Gillen*
www.FredGillen.com

Chapter 5 - Travel
By: Allen Suss

I was born in Melbourne Australia and educated at the local government primary school. I went to Mount Scopus, a top private school, for my secondary education. After secondary college I went to Monash University and studied economics and politics with a little bit of anthropology thrown in.

After graduation I had no idea what I was going to do with my life so I set sail for Sri Lanka (Ceylon in those days) and toured for a couple of weeks with a few friends. Then we sailed on a rudimentary wooden boat that took us, overnight, to the tip of India. We landed at a place called Tuticorin where the local crop was coffee – not tea.

India was such a culture shock for me. I saw people half dressed, strange food, strange sites, cows all over the place and people begging. Such a disorganized place compared with my hometown Melbourne. For me it became the beginning of a great adventure.

I left my friends to travel throughout India and Nepal. Nepal seemed to be similar to India until I got to know it and I realized it was special in its own way. Climbing Tiger Hill and seeing Mount Everest, hidden by cloud, in the far distance was an incredible sight to see. I shared butter tea with Tibetan refugees fleeing from China. The tea was not to my taste!

Travelling was now part of my life so I decided to head for Europe. I flew into Afghanistan in a DC3 aircraft landing in Kabul. A few weeks sightseeing and then I headed for Iran. Some people I met offered me an apartment to stay in. It was in Paris Avenue, in the centre of Tehran. The people I stayed with fed me, took me around the place and directed me to the highlights of the city. They were really nice people. The only thing I regret about my stay in Tehran is I did not take time see the Peacock Throne. The Shah was still on the throne.

My hosts generously gave me a bus ticket to Turkey. It was a two-day, one night journey and ended just over the border. Fortunately for me the police let me sleep in the police barracks overnight as there was nowhere else for me to stay.

I began to realize how travel broadens the mind and offers opportunities to meet people with different outlooks from my own.

My travelling lifestyle lasted four and a half years. For me it was adventure after adventure. I experienced the incredible generosity of people. The way I travelled would probably not happen today. I interacted with people closely enough to learn something of their language in order to communicate with them.

I travelled through Europe on trains and on a Vespa scooter. In England I taught school for a while and on weekends I moved furniture. It was a brilliant way to see London.

At last it was time to go home. My parents lent me the fare home.

Back home, it was time to get serious about my future. For some unknown reason I decided to become an accountant. I joined an accounting firm and became an auditor, one of the most boring jobs in the world. Knowing I was not cut out to be an accountant or auditor I started to look at other options.

My future became clear when my father suggested we form a travel agency using my knowledge of travel in a constructive way.

The travel industry was growing in Australia, gradually allowing more people to become involved. The travel cartel was being challenged. People with old ideas had to look at how travel was opening up. New aircraft with greater speed and capacity were coming on line. New airlines were coming into Australia who all wanted their share of the travel pie. Flight Centre began this era.

All of a sudden younger Australians wanted to travel overseas. Retired people also wanted to travel. The Women's Weekly Tours were incredibly successful at this time. Tour companies with special international tours were growing. A whole new era was opening up.

Our company, The Travel Bag, was situated in an office in Moorabbin, a southern suburb of Melbourne. Computers did not exist in those days so everything we did was manual and looking at manuals. We had no faxes, no telex, no iPods or iPhones. The telephone and sending letters was how we communicated with our clients.

At first we specialized in overland tour packages. We booked people on tours to India and overland to Europe. People preferred to join an organized tour. There was still a certain fear of travelling on your own, by Australians, at the time. Tour companies provided the pioneer spirit for travelers. A lot of our first clientele came from people we knew. My brother, who had also joined Dad and I, had a lot student contacts as well.

We were pioneers in the travel industry but before long we had a lot of competition. To build our business and expertise we worked hard. There were a lot of travel businesses being run by people with lots of experience. Australians were known for their travel expertise and their companies reflected this.

Like most businesses we have had our challenges. In 1980 we were organizing tours to Russia for the Olympic

Games and the Australian Government banned Australians from participating. We couldn't sell our travel packages. Fortunately the Australian Government reimbursed us for any financial losses. We also had issues with some staff members, but overall we were very lucky with the staff we employed.

During the 1970's and early 1980's we had two IATA memberships so we could issue airline tickets from our own office. This was a valuable asset. We sold one for a profit and operated successfully with the other.

There were company changes in the late 1980's. My Father died and my brother Michael decided he wanted to change careers. Labor charges were escalating so I decided to run my agency using the infrastructure of another agency. I did this because there was a lot of back office work and record keeping consuming a lot of my time. I was stayed with this agency for thirteen years.

Without realizing it, I was preparing myself for the next stage. The age of the Internet had arrived. I discovered Travel Managers Australia, a company highly geared to operate in the new Internet age. It was now possible to work from anywhere. I have a great personal relationship with them.

The Information Age has arrived and I have joined it. Clients are able to gain information online on any topic, any place and any airline. With this advance there is now information overload. Al though people are able to book their tickets on the Internet, many have found they are better off using a travel agent.

Like everything there is the good and the bad. More complicated trips are more difficult to book on the Internet. People make mistakes when booking tickets and often do not realize it until they turn up at an airport, cruise ship or tour to find they do not have a booking.

Having joined the Information Age I have been reflecting upon what this means for me as a travel agent. People I now attract are those who want to be confident that all their travel arrangements are done accurately. They want to know they are able to contact me if necessary and for any reason.

You have to be fairly fast on your feet these days to help people travel quickly. People in emergency situations often need seating immediately. For example, recently clients rang me indicating they needed to be on a plane urgently to fly to the other side of the world. They needed to depart in 3.5 hours. I was able to make an instant booking and they met the flight and left on time.

My extensive experience in the travel industry enables me to tailor my client's travel arrangements to their specific needs. If a client needs assistance I have contacts all over the world that can be helpful.

My job is to simplify complex travel arrangements so they appear seamless to the client. My highly personalized service gives my clients something of great value.

I continually educate myself. I am always attending courses, webinars and visiting ships and aircraft to ensure I am at the cutting edge of travel and can confidently advise my clients.

In 2010 I was given an award that recognized me as one of the top ten travel agents in Australia.

The travel group I am associated with, Travel Managers, has an outstanding relationship with all the airlines, shipping companies, tour operators, car hire firms and others related to the travel industry. I am proud that I have very good connections within the industry that I can call upon to be helpful to my clients.

A challenge for clients is to know all the rules and regulations related to visa, passport requirements, duty free allowances, luggage allowances, customs requirements of various countries and much more. As a travel agent it is my responsibility to keep up to date and be able to inform my clients.

I regard my role as still supporting my clients when they are travelling. A recent example of this was when a client of mine was downgraded on a flight from Bangkok back to Australia because the aircraft had been changed. I contacted the client, advised them of the change and offered them a seat on an alternative aircraft that was flying at the same time. The client accepted the change of plans. My clients know I am available outside working hours to issue tickets for them.

Providing the world doesn't blow up or another World War begins I see travel increasing on a much wider scale than today.

Space travel I am sure will happen. Moon visits and visiting other planets is a distinct possibility. Better communications and more internet savvy people will ensure the world becomes better known by millions more than today. Faster and larger aircraft are already being developed.

The wealthy will continue to benefit. I see more exotic cruises happening on sea and land.

Cruise ships will continue to grow in size and attract more and more passengers. The wealthy will have even more luxurious ships and some people may even choose to live on them. Cruise ships, even today, are floating cities with every possible convenience available.

More and more people will be attracted to travelling overland. I can see highways built from Singapore through to Europe for people to use. Cars will not rely on petroleum. They will be solar and battery driven. Buses, motor bikes and bicycles will also be used on these superhighways. It is not impossible for cars to drive themselves and the occupants free to take in the countryside.

For the foreseeable future I will continue as a travel agent aware that I must keep up with all the changes in the industry that are happening at break neck speed. As usual my customers well being will be a primary concern of mine.

Top 10 Travel Tips

1. **Check the latest travel advice** for your destination and subscribe to receive free e-mail notification each time the travel advice for your destination is updated.
2. **Take out appropriate travel insurance** to cover hospital treatment, medical evacuation and any activities, including adventure sports, in which you plan to participate.
3. **Before travelling** overseas register your travel and contact details online or at the local Australian embassy, high commission or consulate once you arrive, so we can contact you in an emergency.
4. **Obey the law.** Consular assistance cannot override local laws, even where local laws appear harsh or unjust by Australian standards.
5. Check to **see if you require visas** for the country or countries you are visiting or transiting. Be aware that a visa does not guarantee entry.
6. **Make copies** of your passport details, insurance policy, travellers' cheques, visas and credit card numbers. Carry one copy in a separate place to the originals and leave a copy with someone at home.
7. **Check with health professionals** for information on recommended vaccinations or other precautions and find out about overseas laws on travelling with medicines.

8. **Ensure** your passport has at least six months' validity from your planned date of return to Australia. Some countries will refuse entry on arrival and some airlines will not allow passengers to board flights if their passport does not meet this requirement. Before travelling, you should contact the Embassy or High Commission of each country you intend to visit to confirm the entry requirements.

9. **Leave a copy of your travel itinerary** with someone at home and keep in regular contact with friends and relatives while overseas.

10. Before departing Australia check whether you are regarded as a national of the country you intend to visit. **Research whether holding dual nationality has any implications for your travel.**

Written by: *Allen Suss - Your Travel Expert*
www.AllenSuss.com

Chapter 6 - Believe in Yourself
By: Liz O'Dwyer

As I sit in my office, looking out onto my gorgeous garden, on this most beautiful spring day in November, I am filled with gratitude. I am wealthy in so many ways.

My business, customer-centricity, is several years old. It is a boutique consulting business, assisting small to medium sized businesses to attract and retain customers. I was recently labelled a Client Attraction Specialist. My office is home based; my home is a 160 year old homestead in regional Victoria. I am blessed. To have the vision to create my own business, build it up to a viable business that is supporting my lifestyle has been a wonderful gift.

It wasn't always like this though. I spent many years travelling by car into Melbourne each day to work. I would spend on average two and a half hours per day in the car. So by Friday night I was exhausted. I would spend the weekend recuperating, only to do exactly the same thing the next week! I was wasting about twelve and a half hours each week sitting in the car. And I was travelling to a job that I detested. The morale was very low; we knew most of the work was about to be outsourced offshore. We also knew that staff redundancies were imminent. These were very difficult circumstances to work under. Everybody was clambering over the top of each other to keep their jobs. I wasn't too worried about my job, because mentally I had already "resigned". I had planned to get a job a lot closer to home. And I already had thoughts about starting my own business. But it was a very interesting time, watching the way management conducted themselves, in what seemed like a dog eat dog world.

This was one of the reasons I wanted to start my own business. To be in control of my own destiny; to be in control of how much money I made each year; to be in control of my own lifestyle; to be in control of who I did business with; to be able to create something much more fulfilling for me on a business level, on a personal level, and all the while assisting other businesses to achieve their goals. I realised there was something better, much more fulfilling in life than "working for the man".

It took me several years to realise that being in business for myself was where I excelled. Several people had said to me over the years, "You should be in your own business". But I didn't see it; not then anyway. It was only after too many years of being employed by somebody else and not getting any job satisfaction that I went out on my own.

Although having a customer service background, it was from a frustrated consumer standpoint that I commenced my business to assist other businesses to attract and retain clients. I am now working with many small to medium enterprises, through courses, workshops and webinars, to assist in building their client base, and ultimately their bottom line sales.

As consumers, we have come to accept mediocre levels of service, and we simply shouldn't. We work hard to earn our money, so our custom should be appreciated and valued by any business.

Ask for Help
When we start out in business we have an in-depth knowledge of the core of our business. However there are so many other aspects to the business that we are not proficient in. Don't be afraid to put your hand up and ask for help. There are people out there willing and able to assist you and they are just waiting to be asked. The biggest compliment we can pay somebody is to ask them to assist you to reach your peak potential. People love to help. It took me a long time to ask for help. Learn from my mistakes. People generally won't know you need

assistance with something. Don't ever assume they know –
ask them.

Outsource the tasks that aren't generating any income.
It's sometimes difficult when starting out, to minimise
whatever business expenses you can. We all do tasks like
administration, bookkeeping, etc, until the money rolls in.
But these tasks are holding us back and slowing down
your success rate. Find somebody you can outsource
these tasks to, so you can get on to the core of the
business and build it to what you want it to be. Barter for
these tasks if you have to, but don't do them yourself.

Get a mentor.
We can't know everything about being in business. Attend
courses and seminars when you can. We never stop
learning. The world is evolving at a very quick pace, so we
need to keep up with the changing faces of marketing,
technology, products, etc.

Network.
People either love it or loathe it. Either way, it's an
essential element for building your business.

Make your business customer centric
Create your business with a focus on your customers. It
will build your business very quickly. You may have a
fantastic product or service; however, if you don't provide
an exemplary level of service, you are hindering your own
success. Take the pressure off yourself, and make your
business customer centric. Did you know that 69% of
customers will take their business elsewhere due to a
perceived lack of interest by the service provider. Don't let
this happen to you.

Take a risk, calculated, but take a risk.
Step out of your comfort zone. Do your homework before
making the leap. Do the market research and ensure it's a
viable business before putting too much energy or money

into the venture. Believe in yourself. Believe in the passion of your dreams and goals. Be crystal clear about the goals you have for your life. And don't let anybody get in the way of them.

Focus your Energy
Pay particular attention to where you place your energy. It's true, "where your focus goes, your energy flows". This means that whatever you are constantly thinking about, you will attract more of. So, if you're focussing on lack of clients, lack of income, lack of success in any area of your life, you will actually be attracting more lack. Focus on gratitude. Focus on what you do have. Focus on the positive. You may have heard the phrase "success breeds success". This is true. Express gratitude for what is already in your life, and you will attract more of the same.

Mix with like minded people.
I've had many "dream stealers" in my life, people who wanted me to stay where I was. And for a long while I believed what they said. I doubted myself and my abilities. So be very conscious about your dreams and who you share them with. These "dream stealers"come in many different disguises, but when it comes to you spreading your wings and achieving your dreams, some people around you can feel threatened. Keep them in your life, certainly, but don't let them stand in your way. Don't let anybody spoil your dreams.

I must say though that if it weren't for those people in my life, I probably wouldn't be here today. I have learnt so much from those people. I have now realised that we learn from all people in our life, even the people that aren't so nice to us. We can learn from these negative people. It was them that taught me about my potential. So, to these negative people, these "dream stealers", I say thank you. If it wasn't for you, I would not have what I have today.

56

My self doubts started me on my personal self development journey. I have completed several self development courses over the years which have helped immensely, both in my personal and business journey. There are so many personal self development courses and professional courses out there – choose one. If you feel limited in any way, ask for help. Be true to yourself. Live the life you were put on this earth for.

Don't get caught up in other people's negativity. I believe we get out of life what we put in. I believe in the Law of Attraction. I believe we all have choices.

Know your business for what it is.
I created this business because there is a need for businesses to focus more on our customers than our bottom line sales. A customer- centric focus in your business is an essential building block. Without it building your business is so much more difficult. By creating a customer-centric business, you'll create a loyal and dedicated customer base who will help grow your business by word of mouth referrals. And these are priceless. This by itself will assist the bottom line sales. You know yourself, as a customer, if you've had a positive customer service experience, you'll tell other people about the business. However, if you've had a negative experience, you'll also tell other people – not to do business with that particular business. It's the same with your customers.

What's Next?
The next step in my journey is to create a property development port folio. I will always have this business, as I love dealing with people, and I love assisting businesses achieve their dreams and goals. And a by-product of them achieving their business dreams and goals is that they then achieve their personal dreams and goals. How cool is that!

So many people have dreams, but they die with them still unfulfilled. I have seen people express their dreams, but they are too afraid to take that first step toward achieving that goal or dream. I have seen others that have had a dream, and a burning desire to achieve that dream, and they have achieved them. Sometimes there will be roadblocks, hardships, stumbles, but there will also be triumphs, blessings, and people who appear seemingly out of nowhere, to assist you on your journey to achieving your dreams. I have been blessed with the people I have in my life.

Maintain work/life balance
Whatever that means for you. Sure, when you first start in your business you will put in longer hours. That's a given. But when the business has found its legs, it is imperative you take time out to re-energise yourself. You can't be putting in 100% of yourself into the business if you're lacking in sleep, a social life, if your mind and body are suffering from lack of exercise and sunshine. Make sure you are, as a business owner, 100% fit and healthy in order to provide 100% commitment to your business and your customers. Who are you not to be the best you can be? What gifts do you have inside you that you are holding back from giving to the world?

I live near the absolutely gorgeous mineral spa township of Daylesford. When I first moved out here I promised myself I would visit Daylesford on a regular basis to reward myself with a massage, or a swim in the mineral baths, or enjoy some of the wonderful cafes, venues and events they have on offer. I very rarely did it. I was too busy with the business. It's only now, after several years of running the business that I can now "afford" the time and money to reward myself for my hard work. It's essential you take time out to reward yourself for goals achieved, both business and personal. This step is ingrained then in your consciousness. So when you set your next goals, you work much harder to achieve them because you know you get rewarded at the end.

My top 5 tips for a successful business:

1. Build a meaningful rapport with your customers. Always be "present" when speaking with them, and really listen to what they are saying. They will know if your focus isn't on them.

2. Maintain excellent time management. This will assist you to achieve more goals, but also to provide a better service to your customers.

3. Value add to your product or service, so the customer always feels valued and appreciated.

4. Always encourage feedback from your customers. This is a fantastic opportunity to improve your service to the customer, thus creating a loyal client base.

5. Make your business easy to find, and easy to contact at all times. Customers won't ring a second time to get hold of you . . . they'll go elsewhere. Remember, if you don't look after your customers, your competitors will.

One of my many favourite quotes, "There is only one success . . . to be able to spend life your own way". *Christopher Morley*

It takes a lot more energy and money to find new customers than it does to retain current ones. So, if you are stuck in your business, or if you are ready to take your business to the next level, you'll need great client retention. It makes the journey so much easier.

If you have a great customer service story and would like to acknowledge a good business and good service, let me know about it and I will post them on the website. Great customer service deserves acknowledgement.

If you would like to contact me, feel free to email me at:
info@customercentricity.com.au

Written by: *Liz O'Dwyer*
www.customercentricity.com.au

Chapter 7 - Where it all began
By: Michelle Hext

I have been in the fitness industry since 1991 with one break along the way. Ironically Glow began after this short stint away from the industry I love so much.

I had gone from owning or partnering in gymnasiums and Taekwondo schools and a personal training studio to setting up a coaching business that led me in the direction of coaching women in small business.

Very quickly I saw just how much health and fitness permeated this arena. As we know how fit, energetic and healthy we need to be to run a business, and particularly a solo business.

Not setting a health, fitness or weight loss goal with a client as part of the coaching series was the exception rather than the rule. Not surprisingly I found this element of my coaching the most enjoyable.

I became quite excited about how much better I would be as a personal trainer and taekwondo instructor with my recently gained coaching skills however the thought of doing personal training hours again didn't appeal to me at all.

When my children were younger it didn't matter so much if I was out in the evenings teaching classes or up and gone early in the morning running PT sessions or opening the gym because I was home with them during the day.

When the kids went to primary school I found I just wanted to be with them in the evenings especially as they got older and wanted to do the usual after school activities.
At this time I was also in preparation for my 4th degree black belt in Taekwondo and was enjoying the challenge of

being fit enough for a 3 hour grading. I also enjoyed encouraging the women I trained with to take up other fitness pursuits outside of taekwondo to support their taekwondo training.

I am in my element when I'm getting people interested in fitness and healthy living and it slowly began to dawn on me that I needed to be doing what I was passionate about and had always been passionate about – I just needed to figure out a better way to do it.

I found coaching a hard slog, not the coaching itself but securing clients; I did the BNI thing and I was also president of a local business group but I am not a sales person and I really hated the element of having to sell myself.

Part of the traditional taekwondo culture is humility and it really went against the grain to have to sell myself to potential clients.

It struck me that in all of my years in the health and fitness industry I had never had to sell myself, clients came easily and readily and I knew from experience that most women were willing to spend money on looking and feeling better.

Selling health and fitness is not hard if you have a good reputation, experience, walked your talk, have good communication skills, a passion for getting your client results and credibility and I had all of those things in spades.

It made me wonder why I ever thought I should do anything else!

Another element I loved about coaching was helping an idea for a business form and become a reality and I really had the bug to start a new business; it was an itch that kept getting stronger and stronger so I began to look into how I could create the perfect personal training business that would allow me to be around my children and not have to work a million hours a week to make a living.

At the time I was running my coaching business and I also was in partnership with another women in an online hub for women in small business.

This was an absolute disaster and we both still shudder at the mistakes we made and how much it cost us, however this business is what gave me the idea to take my personal training business online.

So much of what we were doing online I could translate into fitness.

Over the course of 6 months I played around with different ideas for delivering personal training online until I was pretty confident I knew exactly how I would make this work. When I nailed the business name and had my gorgeous logo created I knew I was on to a winner.

My gut just screamed that this was it – this was exactly the business for me, we were a perfect fit.

Almost 4 years later I still feel the same way.

Lessons I Learned
Luckily for me I got some of the big lessons out of the way in my previous business which meant I avoided making any major mistakes.

Lessons like delegating the work you know you hate or are not good at so you can focus on what you are good at. This means I am much more productive and enjoy pretty much every element of my job and those things I don't enjoy actually get done!

Paying good money for good people where it counts. As an example I have had 2 Virtual PA's and the second and more expensive one spent the first month working for me undoing the mistakes the first (and cheaper) one made.

The art of negotiation and being prepared to walk away. I used to become very attached to an outcome and would often make things happen no matter what! I now understand that there is never just one perfect option.

Trusting my gut, I didn't in the last business, in fact I fought my gut feelings the whole time and if I had listened I would have avoided a very costly mistake.

Successes
The great thing about being a solopreneur is that you don't need to win big awards or make a million bucks to feel successful.

All of the goals, big and small that you set and achieve create a fabulous sense of fulfilment and are extremely meaningful because you know how hard you worked to make them happen.

Being well known and respected in my industry and being sought out for interviews or to speak is always validation I am doing all of the right things but my biggest successes are my clients.

When I change a life through one of my programs words can't describe how proud I feel having done so.

I get to experience this everyday and I never tire of it.

The biggest success would have to be taking this thing that was a vision and creating a successful business from it and along the way helping to define a new industry within the industry.

Another success is creating a business that allows me a lot of freedom and flexibility to be with my family when they need me; the systems I have in place mean the business runs like clockwork.

My business is also completely portable; I have an office but can work from home or anywhere at the drop of a hat.

I went to France to run the Paris Marathon and travelled around France and Italy for 3 weeks, and while my PA ran the day to day operations I was still able to maintain contact with my clients, something that was fun for me (and didn't feel like work) as I could share my holiday with them.

What's Next
The next exciting phase of Glow is to run weekend fitness camps around the country. My first camp is in Melbourne in 3 months with Sydney, Brisbane and Hobart all within weeks of each other.

My clients want to see me face to face and I want to see them.

Remember I have never met my clients; in all of this time I have met 3 clients face to face for a cuppa simply because they lived close enough.

The camps will become a staple part of the business and something I know I will get a real kick out of.

As my kids are older now travelling for a weekend isn't a real problem and I can even take them with me now.

Within the next 12 months I will employ a full-time trainer to help share the client load. The trainer will have a different area of expertise to mine so I can tap into a different section of the market as well.

Tips
Plan for growth in your planning phase so if it comes early you are prepared to make the most of the opportunity.

The way my business runs today is vastly different from the way it began. My systems are much smoother and the delivery of my programs is also different, this was an organic process that took place as I gained more and more clients and had to adapt for higher client numbers than I anticipated.

Because I did anticipate this growth at some stage in the planning phase I could easily roll out my new method of program delivery and client progress reporting as it was needed.

Become a Marketing Guru
The one mistake I did make in this business was becoming lazy with my marketing. I just became so over it and paid lots of money for people to do it for me but never, ever with better results than the ones I got for myself.

I got so caught up in feeling I had to have "the perfect" marketing plan that I spent too much time planning and not enough time rolling it out and I became paralysed by it and this is why I sought help elsewhere. I confused myself and wanted someone to just do it for me!

Once I rolled my sleeves back up and decided to get good at one thing at a time and learn as much as I could about each thing i.e.: blogging, Facebook, Twitter, Google Adwords, Facebook advertising, YouTube channel - I began to enjoy it and found this was the area I could be creative and inspired.

Instead of paying other people to do my marketing I now invest in my own education in this area and the more knowledge I have the more I enjoy it.

Never lose sight of the clients needs.
It took some adapting for me to become close to my online clients as I was with my live clients, taekwondo students or gym patrons.

Because I am an online trainer client contact and attention to detail is even more crucial that it is in a face to face situation because it can be very easy to confuse things or cause offense. You can imagine I am looking at daily exercise and food logs and if the women have had a blow out they are already sensitive to criticism as they have already been beating themselves up over it. I have to be sure I have the right mix of firmness and support so I don't come across as mean!

In the almost 4 years I have been doing this I am happy to say that I have only ever had one miscommunication that caused problems – luckily a quick phone call sorted that out but it reminded me just how clear my communication skills needed to be in this forum.

To compensate for not being with the client each week face to face I needed to create a constant sense of presence in my clients everyday lives and I do this via our reporting process, our online community and by making myself available via phone or email whenever they need me.

I think the fact that we don't see one another face to face means I get a whole new level of honesty; I certainly hear about the good, the bad and the ugly of my clients' weeks.

This is a cliché I know but work hard to make your client feel as though they are your ONLY client; everyone likes to feel special and unique. Think about how you would like to be treated in the same situation and aim to deliver that level of customer service.

Get out and about.
If you are a solopreneur it can be easy to become a hermit. Even more so when you are doing it tough or when things are slow but these are the times you really need to get out and about and be inspired with others or by your industry.

A big high for me is our yearly industry convention and expo. Being exposed to so many others in the industry and to see all the latest and greatest gadgets and concepts is exciting and is like having shot of renewed energy.

If I am feeling alone in my business I start looking for networking events and book in a couple right away. Even if I am not in the mood for networking just being in a room full of other business people and listening to an inspiring speaker is often just what I need to feel connected again.

Move with the times.
Staying current with everything in the fitness industry can be a full time job. Doing a Zumba class to me is akin to torture, but I need to know what this thing is all about so when my clients say they do it or would like to I need to know how hard they are working.

I will go and do different classes or research any new fad if I see it lasting for more than 5 minutes for this reason. If my clients are doing it I need to know how hard they are working and what (if anything) the class or exercise is doing for them.

Staying on top of everything the online world has to offer is also a full time job; every week there is a new social media tool, mobile phone application or web application and it can take a lot of time to be on top of this stuff but it needs to be done so I allocate time each week just to research.

I recently sat next to a woman at a luncheon who was in marketing and I asked her about social media marketing. It was very clear very quickly she didn't have a clue about it.

Social Media Marketing is extremely relevant right now and that this woman had no idea was shocking to me when this is the direction marketing is taking now.

It turns out she works full time and is trying to get her marketing business off the ground at the same time. Obviously a full time job takes up a lot of hours as does staying on top of the ever changing world of social media marketing and there is simply not time for both. I can see a mistake in the making a mile off simply because she is not on top of what is so important in marketing right now. Staying on top of what is relevant in your industry is crucial.

If you can't move a mountain...
Over the past few years I have been invited to cast for various fitness shows; some shows didn't get made, another meant I would have had to go to Sydney (never going to happen with a family) and one I did shoot but it didn't really go anywhere.

I really liked the idea of presenting a TV show but just couldn't seem to make it fit with my business and family so I decided to launch my own TV show called Glow Fit TV. It is still in its infancy and I have a lot to learn but rather than wait around for everything to fall into place I just did it with what I had available to me and who knows what opportunity this may bring in that arena.

Glow Fit TV is a great resource for my clients and a very good way to build credibility. A very inexpensive way for you to showcase your knowledge and talents to help your potential clients know, like and trust.

Survey everything!
Instead of agonising over what you think your clients or potential clients want ask them! Send a survey so you get the answer straight from the horse's mouth. A free e-book

or similar is a good incentive to get them to spend a few minutes on a survey.

One marketing concept at a time
When you begin to unravel the onion that is marketing, focus on one thing at a time; master it then add the next thing.

Don't try to tackle too many new marketing concepts at once because it just becomes too overwhelming.

Take care of your health and wellbeing.

If you crash and burn so does your business so it is really important to give yourself an hour a day to exercise and pack your meals for the day so you have all of the energy you need to tackle your day.

Written by: *Michelle Hext*
www.glowwomensfitnessonline.com.au

Chapter 8 – The Nomad
By: Angela Den Hollander

My name is Angela Den Hollander and I am a successful business woman.

There was a time, though, that I thought I would never be able to describe myself that way.

Let me tell you a little about myself.
I guess I was a born as a bit of a rebel. Something inside me wouldn't settle and I found school very boring. It was dull and repetitive and my whole world felt small and very restricting. After a somewhat nomadic start from Christchurch NZ, then Auckland, I settled with my family in Adelaide which, in those days, seemed to be quite a parochial town. I wanted to spread my wings and take off into a new and exciting world.

I left school at the end of year 10 to go off to art school. My head was full of big dreams of fame and fortune somewhere in the arts; theatre, music... I wasn't too sure, but I knew big things were ahead. We are so passionate about everything at 15, aren't we?

My father had run his own business for years, one of the original 'Mad Men' from the early days of advertising, he then specialised in graphic design, back in the days when no-one really knew what that was. Our move to Adelaide was due to his acceptance of a lecturing post at the only graphic design college in South Australia. Not wanting to deal with endless accusations of nepotism, I chose a different path into the industry by wangling myself into an advertising agency through sheer persistence. I began as the work experience kid who wouldn't leave. I found myself doing the art director's work while he took long lunches. They just couldn't get rid of me so they ended up giving me a job.

The bright lights were still calling me though, so one day I packed up and ran off to Melbourne and started work at Cato Design, a large and quite prestigious design firm. This was a big turning point for me. I learnt a lot about graphic design including what NOT to do.

A couple of jobs later, my career was progressing nicely, from junior to mid and finally senior designer leading a team and working on some prestigious national and international clients, but something was missing. Maybe I just wasn't cut out to be an employee? Something about following others' rules, needing to be physically present and trying to produce great work regardless of my creative state, didn't work for me.

The final straw came when I found myself pregnant with my first child. I had seen and learnt a lot from the way my father ran his business, the way he was able to come to things like my school sports days instead of having to trot off to work as regular employees had to do. I loved that he was able to be available when he wanted to or had to. It seemed to me that self-employment released us from the shackles of the traditional workplace. I was all for freedom, remember. I decided to start up my own business where I could do things my way and do them properly. I wanted to be in control of my business. I was going to be free and able to achieve a balance of working and being there for the little person growing inside.

Well, it sounded good at the time.
Fast forward a few years and here I am married, the mother of a daughter, my gorgeous Matilda, a super bright kid, with all the difficulties that comes with that particular package. Then 4 years later the lovely Aimee joins us and, though I didn't know it to start with, brings with her the extra challenges of Aspergers Syndrome. As a baby she was simply challenging, a rotten sleeper, super-sensitive to loud noises and change.

Two children plus a business as well as taking care of the family, cooking, balancing the family budget and doing all the regular domestic duties of a home-based mum. The sort of workload that needs teamwork, someone to share the burden. Well, that would have been great, but... unfortunately the man I'd chosen to be my life partner was a seriously flawed individual. Stuck in 'employee mindset', bedevilled by fear, he never believed in my business. Every win was a fluke with disaster waiting 'round the corner, every set-back inevitable, and undoubtedly my fault as I was obviously doing something wrong.

The constant criticism kept me stuck, desperately trying to prove myself, make money, be there for the kids, keep the house running, never able to share the normal concerns of any small business owner lest risk another stinging verbal attack about all the ways in which I was doing 'it' wrong, 'it' being whatever took his fancy that day: managing clients, networking, investing in coaching.

Stuck meant knowing that things had to change, but not knowing how. Grow the business so that I could comfortably support my children on my own and leave? Get counselling and stay? I tried it all. Chasing after what I term 'magic pill' solutions – promises of quick and effortless riches, expanding communic8 design with staff and an office, personal development courses like Landmark. If it existed, I tried it.

Meanwhile my ex-husband, the great believer in the security of employee-dom, was fired from job after job. Slowly spiralling downward into lower and lower paying roles.

It was becoming more and more apparent that things couldn't carry on like this. Running a business is hard work, it takes passion, dedication and commitment. Something needs to keep you at it, provide the motivation when it all just seems too hard. For me that motivation was knowing that I had to get out of my marriage and stand on my own two feet. Not just for myself, but for my daughters as well. Not only were they suffering from their father's bullying, critical personality, I was also being a rotten role model.

Luckily for me, my personal epiphany, lead to a business breakthrough. Probably the biggest mistake I made along the way was not demanding respect for my business and for me as a business woman. I realise now that I was guilty of that, too. I didn't invest in myself and I allowed myself to be bullied into treating my work as a hobby. It's very easy to do that when there is a fall back position in the form of your partner's income. It wasn't until I realised that there was no other income stream, in any real sense, that it shook me out of my little rut.

For the first few years I would have to say that like many creatives, I freelanced rather than ran a business. I relied on a handful of large clients that came with me when I started out. I was totally at the mercy of their whims, decisions and corporate takeovers. Yes, I guess I was scared too and there was a degree of safety in sticking with the clients that I knew. I didn't have the confidence to step-up and choose my clients, I let them choose me.

I believe you can run a successful business targeting almost any market. The key is to run a business rather that falling into the trap of being a freelancer though. Freelancers are dependent on others for work, letting the work come to them rather than going out and actively looking for it. Freelancers don't market themselves to find other sources of income. Freelancers have all their eggs in one or two baskets. Freelancers are getting by on good luck rather than good management.

That is a mistake that a lot of new business owners make, particularly service based businesses. They aren't really running a business, they are freelancing, trading hours for dollars, at the mercy of others and vulnerable to competitors. If you want to build a business you need to be out there promoting yourself, networking and positioning yourself as the solution to your target market's problems. When you are that dependent on one source of income and you don't know where your next client is coming from because you don't do any marketing – that's really when you don't have a business.

While starting my business wasn't all plain sailing, I have had the best time. The turning point for me was when I realised that I had been the one who was supporting the family. It made me realise what I was capable of and what my business could become. When I finally listened to myself and started treating the business seriously, it took off. When it is a hobby, you have to justify every hour you use and dollar you spend. If your partner is not supportive, you have to work twice as hard to justify it to him or her. Once you start to take your business seriously it allows you to do so much more. I was free to invest in myself and no longer had to justify the expense. I networked and marketed my business. I invested in my own personal development and I could see it all starting to pay off. I felt like a different person and that had a positive impact on the way I managed my work.

I narrowed my niche so that I could work with the group I really wanted and that was small and micro business. I knew that I would understand what was happening for them because I had been there and faced the same sort of obstacles. We speak the same language. I believe that I charge a price that they can afford to pay so that they can have quality work instead of having to 'make do'.

I now tailor the way that I work so that it frees up more of my time. I have created products, like step-by-step guides, which show businesses how to do things instead of me having to walk each one through individually. Not only does that free up my time but it empowers the businesses to do things for themselves. It gives them the tools they haven't had before but I am still always available if they need me for support. That gives them a choice all the way through. Some business owners want to do it themselves and just ask the odd question. Others need much more support. Creating this choice of options has been really successful for the businesses and for me.

Probably the biggest thing I have learnt is that when you structure yourself correctly and find ways to do things so that you aren't running around like mad, you can empower others and free your time as well. I strive to achieve balance between work and family time, limiting my working hours to around 25 per week while still making enough money to have a good life.

What would I do differently?
I believe that your business comes from knowing who your ideal client is. That might change over time but it's too hard to try to service everyone. They are all very different groups with very different needs and you have very different conversations with each. You can't be everything to everyone. To do that you'd need different websites and marketing materials for each group and that would be very expensive. I don't know that you would end up doing a very good job for anyone. It's so much better to choose one market and focus your efforts there. If I had realised this in the beginning I would have saved myself a lot of time. Become the Go To person for your special area and the work will begin to come to you.

I have also learnt that you need to be strong in business. You need to believe in yourself. If you're mixing with people who are undermining you, you need to have a really good think about whether they should be in your life. We all have enough negative self talk going on in our heads without having it come from your closest contacts, too. There is a saying that says we are the sum of the 5 people we are closest to, so it's always good to have a think about who those 5 people are. Think about whose advice you're listening to.

That also goes for whichever guru you follow. Everyone has slightly different advice to give and I have seen people following one guru then another and another and never actually getting anywhere. A lot of the time we have the answers in place within ourselves and just really need to take the time to listen and trust that we know what is best for us. That is sometimes the hardest lesson of all to learn.

Now that my business has grown and become successful I am moving into a new area. I am moving more into developing fabulous products for businesses which broadens the way I can offer support. My new product is called "Brand Your Business Blueprint" which will show clients how to achieve fantastic results on any budget. Then I will be working on some mentoring projects to help kick start those clients who need a bit of extra support. It's a 10 week program called "Total Brand Aid" which is a done-for-you program with added coaching and mentoring each week. We talk through all sorts of marketing strategies each week and virtually hold your hand as you grow. The aim is to help business owners achieve in 10 weeks what it takes most businesses 1, 2 or even more years to achieve. It's a fast results program.

This is great for me because it lets me share my 16 years of learning and experience with lots of small business owners. I love the idea that they can learn from the mistakes that I have made along the way. I am incredibly proud to think that I can empower business owners in a way that lets them take and keep control over their businesses. I would love to save people some of the heartache that I had to go through along the way.

My top tips for new SMART Business Builders are:
Find your ideal client. I can't stress that enough. Don't keep trying to cater for everyone. Find one market and service it brilliantly.

Build a list as quickly as possible. You need a group of people that you can talk to, who know you, know what you stand for and want to hear from you. Your list is the entry point to your target market so create it as soon as you can.

Brand yourself. Get your branding done right from the beginning so that you make it really clear that you are the Go To person for whatever niche you have carved out.

Be consistent with your branding. A lot of business owners get bored with their look after a while and start fiddling with their colours or shapes. Around the time you're getting bored with it, other people are starting to recognise it. Do you really want to start all over again? A great thing to do at the end of each year is to do a brand check. Print out all your papers and check your web pages too. Make sure the branding is consistent throughout – the same brand in the same size in the same place. Make sure all the contact details are current and correct.. Remember, this is something that people will come to associate with you so you want it to be clear.

Trust in yourself and invest in yourself. Everything in life is a balance. Everything costs whether it's in money or time. Many business owners, whose partner doesn't believe in them, end up spending incredible amounts of time doing things instead of investing money into their business. Faster results come from investing the money. Someone has always done it before and is willing to show you how to do it for a small investment.

Outsource, outsource, outsource. Only do what you can do. We always think of the money but you have to think about your time too. As they say, time is money so why waste it on doing something that you are not good at? You'll take ages to get it done and end up with only an average result. There are many things that I outsource now because I just don't have the time to do them and it gets me far better results

No matter what you do, the important thing is to have passion for what you are doing and follow your dream. That's what I did and I am still following it today. It is taking me to some really exciting places and bringing me new opportunities every day. I wake up every morning and look forward to my day. I know that no matter what happens, I can support my girls and myself and provide for our futures. That gives me so many choices in life that I didn't have. I can't imagine ever giving that up. Yes, I think the rebel is still alive inside me and she is pushing me to be the self-sufficient person I started life as. I might have been a wild child at 15 but I think she knew the best way through life.

Whether you have read this through or skipped to the final paragraph, I want you to take this point seriously. Step up and take yourself and your business seriously. Don't let anyone or anything hold you back. Don't rely on your partner's income; you never know what's around the corner.

Written by: *Angela den Hollander.*
www.communic8design.com.au

Chapter 9 -The Cartridge Family
By: Danielle Storey

Escaping the corporate world is a dream for many working Australians and David and I were no different.

By 1997, David had spent 20 years in credit management and I had spent 10 years in internal sales and marketing. I also sold party plan products and worked part-time in the catering and fashion industries.

We decided to buy a Tattslotto agency and ran that for 2 years before making a quick sale and escaping. It was exceptionally long hours for very little daily return. Owning a Tattslotto business is similar to owning a McDonald's restaurant; it's not the daily profit that you buy it for, but the long term gain when you sell it. We loved serving our customers, who came from far and wide to have fun with us, but the one intolerable factor was armed hold-ups. On one occasion our kids were in the back room, and had it gone horribly wrong, they would have been in serious danger. We both still have a wariness about us when we go into banks and other Lotto outlets and we will never willingly operated a retail business again as a result of the hold-ups.

After escaping the agency, we had only a little money to invest in a new business. We had used all of our superannuation and much of our available equity to buy the agency.

David particularly wanted a business that sold consumable products. We had already owned a business in gambling, that left food, sex and stationery. We looked at a number of food businesses, but having come out of an industry that consumed an enormous amount of our time, we decided we wouldn't enjoy early morning deliveries. Of course, for us the sex industry wasn't really an option, so that left stationery.

David approached his niece, Joanne and nephew, Darren and they agreed to buy with us a franchise in cartridge refilling. We agreed that Jo and I would keep working for other people, to keep money flowing in, whilst the boys built up our cartridge empire. Unfortunately, as some franchise owners find, the decision to buy that particular franchise led to dramas and problems and we bailed within 12 months.

At the suggestion of Joanne's friend, we re-named ourselves The Cartridge Family. Right from the very beginning we were excited about our company name. It is such fun. When we phone people that haven't heard of us before, we often get a moment's silence, or a snigger as they remember wonderful The Partridge Family.

Very early on, David and Darren realized that refilling cartridges was not particularly fun. Both homes were filled with the black dust so they found an external company who was refilling cartridges who could supply what they needed and The Cartridge Family became a distribution company. They mainly sold refilled (or remanufactured) cartridges, but they also sold some genuine cartridges too.

Over the past 11 years, the mix of compatible to genuine product sales has changed considerably. Today, less than 1% of cartridges we sell are compatible or remanufactured. Many businesses in Australia prefer the ease of buying and using genuine toner and ink.

In addition to toner and ink, we also dabbled in paper and register rolls, and we currently distribute labels but our niche has always remained in toner and ink. We also recommend and sell printers, but do so at such a low margin and do so to provide a valuable service to our customers. After all, there are very few companies

81

focusing on selling printer hardware that suits the customers' needs and costs the least amount possible.

Joanne fell pregnant with twins about 4 years into our business partnership. We were still really struggling to make a profit. We had gone to half wages too, and I was working a number of part-time jobs to make ends meet. It wasn't a fun time for any of us.

I remember during one evening meeting between the four of us, we decided to undertake two new initiatives to see if we could change our fortune. One was to "give back" by regularly donating to a charity (we chose to sponsor a child from Senegal with World Vision). The other was to begin networking at local business networking events.

Not long after that, Darren and Joanne left the business and David and I committed to continue on our own. Darren and David are both fabulous detail- and process-oriented people. But what the business needed was a sales and marketing person to grow sales. David and I agreed that I should give up my part-time work (I was working with children with autism and also working in a primary school as an integration aide) and come into the business full-time to telemarket and undertake marketing initiatives. We would continue our sponsorship of Anta, from Senegal (we still sponsor her today) and I would undertake the networking initiatives that Darren had talked about.

I soon discovered that I hated telemarketing. Many companies in the industry were doing it and I wasn't getting a great reception from my prospects (surprise, surprise). So I avoided doing it completely and ultimately we decided that we didn't want our reputation to be sullied by the underhand tactics that our competitors were using. For the past 5 years we have never telemarketed a customer.

Fortunately, I also discovered that I loved networking. After all, networking involved food and coffee and talking, all things that I am good at. Over the years I have attended a number of local networking groups, namely the Knox Business Referral Network, BNI (Business Networking International), Breakthrough for Breakfast, Melbourne Business Golf Group and OzChild Unite. Today our greatest networking revenue is generated from BNI and I am proudly a 5 year member.

Networking is a marvellous opportunity to grow both the individual and the business. I always used to think that a successful networker had to be outgoing and talkative. I mean, I am outgoing and talkative, so I thought I would make a great networker. I learned very quickly that those that talk too much are generally selfish networkers - always trying to sell themselves or their product. I learned that introverted people make much better networkers because they already know how to listen to other people and they generally take an interest in the other person.

As a result of networking, I learned how to listen, and how to ask the right questions. I also learned how to become a conduit, a connector of people as a result of listening and asking the right questions.

One of the networking gurus of the world, Ivan Misner the founder of BNI, in his book The 29% Solution, teaches that as a networker you should approach a networking event as though you are a host. You should direct people to food and facilities and introduce people to each other. People are then drawn to you, your intentions change and you develop an air of helpfulness. People remember you and are willing to build a relationship with you. [1]

---

[1] Misner, Ivan R. with Donovan, Michelle R., *The 29% Solution: 52 Weekly Networking Success Strategies*, Austin, Texas, Greenleaf Books, 2008

This is how I network. For me, networking is still fun, and it is still a great way to grow our business.

In the beginning of my networking journey, at the same time, a major retail customer of ours was growing too, so our turnover was growing rapidly. Simply put, our gross turnover began to look fabulous. What we (I) didn't pay attention to was the deeper figures of the business, until it was almost too late. We nearly lost our major customer and in assessing the balance of the business, we saw that the sales of the major customer represented over 75% of our turnover and our profit margin for them was tiny. (We had the proverbial "eggs in one basket" scenario.) That was a scary couple of weeks. We kept the customer, but made a commitment to finding other customers to provide the balance.

In the meantime, I have to admit (very quietly, mind you), I wasn't really working effectively. I have the "Star" personality profile. I love to flit about and meet people. I was great at promising wonderful things and not so great at following through when the work, or the promise, got boring.

I had battled this problem for all of my working life, and if the truth be written - for all of my life. I consistently signed up for, or committed to many new and exciting things to keep me interested, but then, when I got overloaded, or I let down too many people down, I bailed and failed.

I "enjoyed" the unhealthy process of distraction. Every time things got hard for me (I had to work hard, or I had to address some of my issues attached to rejection or boredom) I found something new to get excited about and committed to, and turned in a different direction, leaving a trail of unfinished work and projects in my wake.

Again, surprise, surprise, this drove David nuts. As a process oriented worker and personality, he couldn't understand why I couldn't just dig in and work hard like he did. What I really needed was outside accountability. I was too stubborn to be accountable to David, so I decided that I needed a coach.

I had met many coaches in my networking journey. We didn't have a lot of money in the business in those days, so we didn't feel we could seriously entertain the idea of paying a coach, and David didn't understand why I needed one. Every one of the coaches I met could see the potential in the business and the potential in me. Some of them offered to coach me for nothing.

Visualize me avoiding the phone call of one (free) coaching individual following up on his request that I telemarket some new customers. You might laugh, I do in hindsight, but it was easy for me to avoid him, there was no pain in the avoidance for me.

Eventually, I met Stefan Kazakis at a breakfast briefing for Action Coach. I had no intention of going, as I had previously looked at Action Coach as a potential coaching option and dismissed it, after all they are not the cheapest coaching option available. I arrived late (a sabotaging tactic?) and took the last seat in the room, next to Stefan. I networked with Stefan and with the guy on the other side of him and had a lovely morning. In that short 2 hours, I knew that Stefan could be a person I could be accountable to. He came and negotiated with David and I, and by lunchtime we (I) had a coach.

The very first thing Stefan did was make me assess the numbers of the business. I say "made me" but really, we agreed that I had a lot of things that needed uncovering for our business to be a success. He made me determine numbers such as our profit margins, our average dollar sale and our break even day. All of these numbers took me by surprise. Suddenly I knew what each new customer cost me to obtain, or what their first sale average would be.

We could then start planning knowing real numbers, not just numbers we "thought" might be.

Throughout that first year of coaching Stefan and I only ever talked business, strategies and business relationships. As you might imagine, working with my husband wasn't always easy (I say that; David says working with me wasn't easy!). Suddenly I had someone I could vent to, in a business sense, and someone who could give me real and diplomatic responses that I could use in the tense situations that arose (regularly). It worked wonders for our relationship. In addition, I was finally working, in a process-oriented manner that meant David was under less pressure to shoulder the entire load in the office. That worked wonders for our relationship too.

Another added bonus was that I felt good about myself. I no longer hid behind my distractions (well that didn't happen overnight, but it did happen!) and found that I was achieving things that I didn't know I could. The non-major customer figures, which I became responsible for tripled over a two year period. I was no longer a "gunna", but an achiever.

Today, we are still being coached by Stefan. Of course we make all of our business decisions ourselves, but we often run marketing and major initiatives past Stefan. After all, he has run major businesses of his own, successfully, and he works with multitudes of other businesses that undergo similar challenges that we undergo.

For the first 7 years, the business operations were based in our front formal lounge room. Often we couldn't see out the window for the piles of cartridges and paper. At one stage, reams of paper were stacked up and down the hallway to the bedrooms. Finally, we realized that we had to do something. At the time we couldn't afford to rent a factory, so we built a garage and professional office off the back of the garage to work out of. It cost us $10,000 to build and fit out.

The biggest gain was being able to walk away from the business when we finished for the day. Previously, when it was in the lounge room, David would wander into the office on a Sunday morning to check the soccer results and end up responding to email or processing orders. When the office was outdoors, our private time stayed our private time. (I like to tell him that his laziness overrode his dedication.)

The second gain was that we had room to employ some staff. Just prior to employing Stefan, we employed a contract sales person. There were a hundred reasons why he didn't achieve any sales, but when it came down to it, it was a bad move for us and cost us a lot of money we didn't have to waste. Stefan immediately coached us to let the salesman go.

As you might imagine, we were reluctant to dip our toe in staffing waters again, but we had to, to grow. With Stefan's help we drafted an advertisement for an internal sales person, part-time, and interviewed. We were set to employ a lady who was lovely, but not perfect for our needs, when Stefan told us to go to a second and third interview to make sure. At the very last minute, the lovely Natasha decided to apply. We were over the moon when we recognized a perfect fit for our business and our culture. She is a mum and wanted to work part-time to be available for her children. She is clever and personable and fun.

In the office, we have a lot of fun. It is a small space where laughter occurs and funny quips are spoken often. A culture fit, with staff, is incredibly important to us. Culture, to us, translates as the attitudes and expressions of person within the collective group. Culture is something that a single person can affect, but not create. Our culture is one of utmost service, to the customer and to each other. It is having fun in the office, and being open and honest. It is never nasty and often fun.

Natasha helped us transform The Cartridge Family. With Natasha's help, we devised many new or improved initiatives to spoil our customers. We call it our "Customer Delight System". We send birthday presents, we make sure that we consistently follow up with potential customers with a hand written card, and we supply our famous lolly frogs with every invoice.

Today, there is so much to be proud of.

The Cartridge Family ships supplies ink, toner and printers out of warehouses to businesses across Australia and New Zealand. We spoil our customers whenever we can and focus primarily on serving.

We have a family friendly attitude towards our staff. David and I have children (four that range from 24 to 10) and we know how hard it is to work happily when our primary focus is our family. Many employees and business owners feel that they have to sacrifice one for the other; work for family or vice versa. We aim to ensure that our employees don't feel this way.

We also have a wonderful part-time worker (another mum) who packs all of our orders and have just employed another wonderful mum to work full time with us as an internal sales person.

We are in the process of buying our first factory/office and intend to create a kids room. We envision that the room will be filled with fun things for kids to do, not because we expect our staff to come to work when their children are sick, but to provide an option at school holiday and other times if they wish.

We have already ticked off some major goals that we have been aiming for. One of those goals is to travel extensively, every year. Last year we took a two week holiday (our first in 10 years). With our youngest daughter we visited Disneyland in California for a week and relaxed for a week in Mexico. This year, 2011, we have booked four weeks in the UK, to spend time with our eldest daughter who is living there.

The cartridge industry is massive all across the world. In Australia there are hundreds of cartridge suppliers. We know that the industry has room for all the great operators, like us, and have no concerns about "lack" or "scarcity". We enjoy communicating with other fabulous cartridge suppliers and swap information and communication often.

Testimonials that come in regularly, telling the world how wonderful our service is. It is a tall order, delighting every single customer, but it is a goal that we will continue to have and aim for. We aim to own The Cartridge Family for many years to come. One of the key concepts that Stefan taught us was that Management, in any business, is responsible for the wellbeing and performance of the staff of their business. Following on, the staff is responsible for the delight of the customers. The customers are responsible for the success of the business and the business is responsible for the wellbeing of the management. It is a simplistic, circular view, but like all great concepts, the simplest are the most effective and profound. We will certainly be spending the future looking after our staff, so that they can continue to wow our customers.

After all, our tagline is, "We'll Look After You".

Written by: *Danielle Storey*
The Cartridge Family 1300 1 TONER (1300 186 637)

Chapter 10- Idealism
By: Karina Butera

The impetus

When asked why I started High Ideals, I always suck in my breath and feel my cheeks heat up in embarrassment. My reason is so simple – too simple – and ridiculously idealistic.

I was battle weary from operating in a business world of game-play, pretence and double standards. I wanted to do business with good people, only good people. In order to do this, I wanted to band a bunch of good small business people together to have a fair chance of succeeding alongside the big businesses (and the small businesses with big business clout).

When I say 'good' I mean 'good' in every sense of the word. There are many who are 'good' at what they do technically, but they aren't so good at being nice about it. I wanted to connect and work with people who were not only good at their trade, but who I could count on and who were 'good' to do business with. I wanted to connect and promote 'good people' doing 'good business'.

Although I was playing a crusading role of sorts, my motives shouldn't be seen as entirely altruistic. In fact, the truth is, I was disgruntled and really just wanted to hide away in a small business gold fish bowl rather than exposing myself in the dark deep ocean with the sharks. So it was out of self-preservation that the decision to start High Ideals was made.

My experience, after years of study, diligence, getting good results with the few clients I had and working long hours was rather disappointing. I expected that having worked hard, being honest and caring about my work and clients and having a fair bit of skill in my profession that clients would be knocking my door down.

They weren't.

Yet, when I went to networking and industry events I was literally horrified to hear others in my profession spouting off about how many clients they had and the exorbitant fees they charged. To me these people seemed to have far less experience, professionalism or credibility than me. In fact, they used various techniques that we are taught in professional coaching (neurolinguistic programming for example) to play mind games and gather a following and guru status with the most cliché of promises.

Exploring the idea
Having a social research background, I started to do my own pseudo research project, mentally noting who were the people with the supposed material success in small business and who were the ones struggling. It didn't take long to realise that it was the humble ones, those who weren't so good at blowing their own trumpets, those who were honest, caring and willing to go the extra mile who seemed to be peering out from the shadows.

So my journey to begin High Ideals started with some probing conversations with these 'like-minded' people. The discussions normally started with me saying 'what do you think of about a dozen of us all getting together, putting in $500 a year each and putting an ad in the BRW advertising us as a group of good people to do business with?"

All agreed, and the idea had budded. It wasn't something I threw myself into initially without reservation. In fact, I'd virtually thrown out the idea (in a rather pathetic bout of self-pity) by the time I had a spur-of-the-moment brunch with my dear friend and fellow idealist, Noel Posus on a Sunday morning in September 2008. As I kept throwing him reasons my idea wouldn't work, he kept asking me 'why not?' My final answer to that question was 'because I don't have a name for it, no matter how hard I try – nothing I can think of even slightly communicates the high ideals that the name needs to encapsulate!'

Noel looked at me with an eyebrow raised and a grin that told me the answer was sitting right there in my statement. And after checking availability of business names and websites, High Ideals was born.

The next step was to really nut it out conceptually. I wrote up a simple six page conceptual document and sent it to eight trusted colleagues, the document ending with three questions:

Does this idea have legs?
Are you convinced enough to be a member?
If so, are you convinced enough to help me get it started?
Incredibly I got a 100% response rate of yes, yes, YES!

The feedback was 'go bigger', 'go national'- for this to have impact, it needs numbers. As a result I revisited the business plan and hiked up the numbers, nodding in satisfaction when I saw how that positively impacted the bottom-line of the business.

So my original 'small' idea grew a lot bigger.
Originally I wanted High Ideals to be about the members – a cooperative of sorts. I had mooted the idea of a not-for-profit organisation. Several of my trusted founding advisors felt this was unwise – they had seen many people put their souls and wallets into NFPs only to have them fall flat due to volunteer-fatigue and lack of funding. The feeling was that the business would not be taken seriously and that it should actually be a profit making business.

The leap of faith
So I started the business as a company and invested thousands of my own dollars into the set up. The more people started hearing about the venture, the more I was offered help. At that stage I was unable to pay anyone, so they all agreed to volunteer until revenue appeared.

Before long we had a team of 15 specialists – ranging from quality assurance to IT, events management to accounting. We were all excited, motivated and loving the feeling of belonging to a team of such positive, integrity-driven people.

With no money to spend on marketing, we used our personal networks to 'spruik' High Ideals, and offered extended membership to founding members. By the time we officially launched the business in July 2009 we had approximately 50 members, which was a meagre attempt at my original goal of 200 by launch.

Although the original idea had gotten bigger, the reality wasn't nearly as big as I had hoped.

The main benefit we were delivering to our members at this stage was a monthly newsletter providing information to our members in a set format that focussed on promoting members, educating them on ways to have a more positive impact and providing links to inspiring resources and websites. We were also holding regular 'gatherings' in Melbourne and Sydney where members were able to share experiences and ideas. Because of our low numbers, there were only ever a handful of members at each gathering.

Although the membership numbers were well below my hopes and expectations, those who had joined were getting great value from their membership and excellent relationships and referrals were being created between members. I received emails on a weekly basis telling me how grateful members were to me for creating my vision. The emails of appreciation and encouragement spurred me on over the months ahead as, try as we may, the numbers simply did not grow.

The challenges
Not only were our member numbers not growing, our management team numbers were shrinking. While it had been exciting to be at the forefront of a new venture, the commitment required from the team, without pay, was paying a toll, and slowly volunteer-fatigue set in.

One of the biggest problems we seemed to encounter was that many had a 'passion' for the venture, but not the specific skills or connections required to raise awareness and bring in members. Others had the desire to learn new skills but we did not have the time or trainers to help them develop these skills. Those with skills ended up shouldering much of the work, which took them away from their 'paying work', and they soon had to set boundaries.

A further problem we dealt with is that our management team spanned four states of Australia, so the majority of meetings were held over telephone link up – which hindered full communication and relationship building between team members.

Regardless of reducing our fees, increasing membership periods and adding further benefits, within six months of our launch our membership numbers had barely grown and our contributing team had shrunk to a third of its original size.

In January 2010 we had our first strategic planning session. I flew two of our key management team members to join the other three key members in Melbourne. They stayed at my home for the weekend, sharing kitchen and bathroom, and spreading across the dining room table with laptops, chocolate biscuits and iced water over the two day session.

It was a full agenda by day, which spilled over into the evening festivities on my back patio by night.

Within the first hour of the first day we had faced reality, exposing a very tender nerve for me. I sat at the table with my four 'die-hard' colleagues and choked back tears as I admitted that I did not have much hope or energy left for High Ideals. After the tissue box had been passed around, we made a pact that if we could not come up with a decent strategy to save High Ideals, we would allow it to be gently put to sleep.

One hour later a whole new energy had been created.
A strategy to engage youth was suggested and suddenly a whole new dynamic was created. It meant bringing in a more holistic model, focussing not only on small business, but on the actual idea of promoting, educating and rewarding high idealism. By the end of the weekend we decided our vision was to split the organisation into five divisions: individuals, business, youth, caring causes and the natural environment.

We left the meeting excited and motivated about the new direction, however, what we hadn't realised is that this new strategic direction effectively quadrupled our focus, and with such a small team, we all started feeling a little schizophrenic as we tried to keep our eyes on five balls as opposed to one. Added to that, although it had always been a challenge to explain the concept of High Ideals to others, now it was even harder, and giving an 'elevator pitch' became near impossible.

Over the months that followed, with few members signing up, I came again to a cross-roads. With such limited human capital, we were still struggling to get our tasks completed. Three compounding factors had become clear:

The longer we went without bringing in more members, the more fatigued the team were getting and the more work I had to take on.

The more work I took on, the less 'paid' work I was able to do in my two other businesses, and all business development was focused on High Ideals as opposed to my profit making businesses.

Those who were continuing to work were doing so as paid contractors (even if the rates were low compared to market) and each month I pumped more money into the business.

Letting go and letting good
My bookkeeper, Leigh, sat me down one afternoon in April 2010 and gave me a serious talking to. He pointed out the issues I'd been trying to ignore and forced me to come out of my denial about the financial reality of the business.

I didn't like it! I recall becoming extremely defensive and passionately angry. I was honest with Leigh about that, which was obvious anyway because I could feel the heat from my face, so it must have been scarlet and my voice was pitched to a level that would shatter glass. Fortunately Leigh knew me well enough not to take offence to my defensiveness and he reminded me that he was telling me this out of care of me and fear for me if I continued on the path I was on.

Because I had never taken too much notice of the financial side of matters, I asked Leigh to let me know how much money I had invested in High Ideals over the 18 months I'd been running the business. When he told me how much I was flabbergasted! I had no idea I had sunk so much of my own cash into High Ideals.

It's worth noting at this point that three months prior to launching High Ideals in 2009, my marriage had ended.

So having let go of the security of having a 'breadwinning' husband, I now had to face reality that I could no longer keep throwing money at High Ideals.

My heart was struggling with the reality of the situation.
How could I let go of something that had meant so much to so many? By now we had more than 80 members, half a dozen ambassadors, and we were making a difference in many areas in small ways. I felt a deep sense of responsibility to these people; yet, I could not ignore the fact that for every day I kept High Ideals operating, I was financially, physically and emotionally going further and further backwards.

I'm not one who likes to give up. People would not necessarily refer to me as a control freak, but I certainly will not usually jump ship at the first sign of danger. However, at that point I realised that for High Ideals to survive, the members had to save it.

I spoke to the management team first and posed the idea of changing the corporate structure to non-profit. Once they had all the facts, they were fully supportive. When I shared my sense of 'leader's fatigue' with Noel he agreed to step into the driver's seat should the members agree with the decision. Although there were some members who asked questions about the why's and how's, I was touched to receive email after email of gratitude to me for bringing High Ideals to this level and support for the vision regardless of whether it was driven by me or a Board.

The pragmatics of the switch were far less simple. My accountants had to fiddle my businesses around in a complex way in order to make the change happen. Despite the challenges, in July 2010 High Ideals Pty Ltd became High Ideals Ltd with a Board of three: Noel Posus, as Chairperson, myself as Vice-Chairperson and Secretary, and Stephanie Noon as Director of Marketing.

Now all we had to do was fill the seven empty seats on the Board and top up our management team, plus change over our entire quality management system (more than 100 documents) to comply with NFP regulations.

Oh, yeh, let's not forget, find more members. No small set of tasks!

It always amazes me in life that when I begin trying to cling and control, things get stuck, yet when I let go, things flow. As soon as I let go of High Ideals, the flow began. One of our 'die hards', Julie Saunders, who has been my support and right hand person from day one, was selling a house and used a real estate agent, Raman Arun, who was 'high ideals quality'.

She brought him to a gathering and he immediately joined the HI Community. He then introduced me to John McCann, who was the founder and leader of Helper Agent. John and I hit it off immediately and set to work assisting each other. Before long John was appointed to the Board with responsibility for the Individual Membership portfolio and we had struck a deal to reward Helper Agent members through free assessment.

Quickly we started to see membership applications come through from Helper Agents.

It took several months but we have slowly added more people to our board, and they are people who share the passion – people who feel as privileged to be part of the venture as I feel privileged to have them as part of it. Further, more people have been brought in by these board members as management team members and committee members.

As of 5.06pm Sunday 28 November 2010, we have 111 members spanning six countries, a dozen ambassadors, a dozen on-call volunteers and business advisors, five management team members and six board members. We have linked and assisted many other not-for-profit organisations who we are able to help have a broader positive impact.

We are in the midst of planning our first Awards Ceremony for 2011 and already have our first Award named and sponsored. Our members continue to express gratitude and honour to be part of this very special community. The best thing is that I am now having people call or email me, telling me about how they are spreading the word and bringing people into the High Ideals community.

There are many other alliances that have been made which are poised to see rapid growth and broader impact for High Ideals, which is extremely exciting.
There is more growing to do and much 'good' work ahead, including initiating our consumer-driven marketing campaign, seeking government funding and commencing our youth rewards program.

So when I was asked to write for this book I felt slightly 'unproved', but upon reflection, I realise that this business has indeed been a success. Why? Because what started off as an idea that stemmed from a disgruntlement not only for myself but for all those who suffered for their integrity, has now taken on a life of its own. It no longer belongs to me – High Ideals is for all those who care, and care about those who care.

It gives a collective 'hip hip hoorah' and sense of community to those who don't just pin their values on their reception wall, but practice them daily in a constant effort to make a difference to the world.

Momentum has taken place and the impact will continue long after my own voice is absent.

That, to me is success - not money, not celebrity, but knowing that I can go to my grave having acted on a vision that had persisted to nag me to create; to have sought out and found those like-minded friends-in-business who shared the dream and joined forces with me to bring it to life. That vision has now taken on a life of its own. I look forward to the day that there is as much understanding of and respect for the High Ideals three ticks of accreditation as there is of the heart foundation tick, finally giving the 'good' people in business the recognition and road to success that they are so worthy of.

If there is a business you would like to start, I hope my story will inspire you to action. I am no business guru; I'm just a person who was compelled to take action on her inner frustration. So if you have something deep inside that stirs you, it most likely will stir someone else; if it stirs someone else, it most likely will stir many; and if it stirs many, it has the potential to make an enormous difference to the world in which we live – so who are you not to take action on what stirs you?

Lessons
What I've discovered and learnt to trust in business is:
Create a business based on something you feel deeply passionate about and has personal meaning to you.
Develop a group of trusted peers in a variety of professions who can offer you a range of perspectives on your ideas, challenges and solutions.

Seek first to give – to meet the needs of others, and then they will gladly come to your aid when you need it.
When you have an idea, do your homework and take your time in developing it – understand it fully yourself before you 'pitch it' to others.

Stay optimistic, but be ready for setbacks.
See your business plan as a 'work in progress', be prepared to adjust it over and over and over again.

Always show gratitude for the assistance you get – no matter how small.

Collaborate and celebrate!
Be realistic without being pessimistic - keep company with those who are positive and supportive (avoid overly critical people and 'know it alls').

Listen to advice, but don't act on it without a second or third opinion.

When in doubt, make a decision and act on it – which beats making no decision at all!

There will always be someone who disagrees with you, understand that a decision isn't necessarily wrong because of this.

Understand the difference between tenacity and stubbornness.

Know when to let go.

Written by: Karina Butera
www.high-ideals.com

Chapter 11 - Life's Lessons
By: Tania Smith

When I started Typengraphics 2 years ago, it was going to be a small "hobby" business that I could do on the side while I look after my two children under 2. Never in my wildest dreams did I expect it to turn into what it has today.....

When I was 10 years old, I clearly remember telling my Mum that when I grow up I want to be an Entrepreneur. I didn't really know what the word meant – but it sounded important! I was a pretty good student at school and did very well in my Year 12 Small Business Management class – in fact our business (which was a telegram delivery business called "Risky Business") continued long after I finished Year 12. It only ceased to exist as I went off to study a career in media and face the big wide world of business.

Deep down I always knew that I'd eventually own my own business – I just had a lot of "life lessons" to learn before I got there. My employment background is chequered. I've done everything from cleaning toilets, to running a caravan park, to running offices, reception work, temp work, assistant store manager, retail...You name it, I've probably done it. I found that I tended to get "bored" after 2 years. Not a good look on your resume!

But as I went through all these employers I began to realise... I'm just as smart (if not smarter!) than some of these people. So I began to question "Why aren't I running my own business?". I could begin to see patterns forming in the type of people I worked for and knew that I was in those jobs for a reason – there was a lesson I had to learn.

During those times I discovered that some people didn't like it when you made suggestions on how they could improve systems on their business, or change their branding slightly to match their target market (well they did ask for my opinion!) so being someone who doesn't like to rock the apple cart I learnt to keep my big mouth shut and become a "yes" woman, but I made sure I learnt what I could and filed details away in the back of my mind.

The years passed and I began working in a major retailing clothing store in a capital city. I had been promoted to an assistant manager after 3 months and was also in line to travel around Australia teaching store employees how to use the new computer systems. This should have been a fantastic time in my life – but I was terribly unhappy. My fiancé (now husband) and I had talked previously about packing it all in and going on a travelling holiday.

One day I'd had enough. I clearly remember being stuck in traffic on my way to work (which was way over the other side of the city) and getting very agitated. I then yelled out "That's it. I can't and won't do this ANYMORE!". So that day I set the wheels in motion to leave the city and head Outback. I was so determined to leave that I said to Scott (my fiancé) I'm going whether you go or not – thank goodness he came too! Five weeks later we were off.

Leaving the city life behind for a life on the road is the best thing one can do for cleaning the soul. We ended up travelling in our 1967 Franklin Caravan and our old Pajero for two years through the top of South Australia, to the Northern Territory and into Western Australia. We had the time of our lives. One thing that really struck me is that, up there no one cared who you were, what you did, where you came from or how much money you had. Everyone was treated the same – it was a totally eye opening experience. It gave me more confidence in myself and a belief that I never knew existed.

After 2 years we'd had enough (see the pattern!). We were working in an Aboriginal community store in WA and had only been there for three days. One morning we woke up and one of our dogs (who managed to win us over) had gotten out and was stirring up a guest trying to get to the toilet. When we had taken on the job we were promised a number of things that no one seemed to know about when we got there (which was stressful enough). One of them was a secure place for us to let our dogs run around.

The stress of that, coupled with a distraught women running around the toilet block in her dressing gown screaming because this over excited dog was jumping and licking her was all too much. We quit our job on the spot and travelled home.

We decided to move to Victoria and see if we could find a nice house to buy and "settle down". Well, within four weeks of moving we were the proud owners of an old cottage on an acre block in country Victoria!

Now that we had a mortgage, it was time to go back to work. My first job was working as an office manager in a wheat collection point. I had never had to weigh trucks on a weigh-bridge before or read what the current wheat prices are to people over the phone, but I soon learnt and I was back into the swing of things.

Unfortunately that job was only for a season, so I had to look again.

This time I took a job at a service station. Although the work was ok, that fire in my belly started to reignite and I KNEW that I could do better.

After about 6 months I left that job and went to work at the local paper/printers. That was quite interesting as all the skills I learnt in my past jobs and training were finally put to use. Unfortunately it only increased that fire in my belly – I KNEW I had to do something.

So I moved through another two jobs – working for an animal welfare group and then for a local farm machinery manufacturer. Both jobs had their own sets of challenges and again made me realise that I need to do my own thing. I could see where things could be improved, but again none wanted to listen so I kept my mouth shut.

It was at this time that I realised I was pregnant. A bit daunting in itself! I decided that then was a good time as any to start my own business.

Well, let's just say it failed dismally. Not only for lack of planning, but also for lack of passion. I decided to put everything on hold and concentrate on being a good mum!

During the first year of my gorgeous son's life I resigned from and went back to the same part time job twice (as people kept resigning). I then gave birth to my beautiful daughter – and 3 months later I got the phone call again asking if I could come back to the same part time job as someone else had resigned.

I stupidly agreed.

It wasn't long before I'd had enough. I could still see the same things happening in the business and I just couldn't handle it. It was enough to get me working SERIOUSLY on my new business.

On November 21, 2008 Typengraphics was born. It took us ages to decide on a business name. In the end we chose Typengraphics as I was going to be offering Virtual Administration Services (type) and graphic design services (graphics). We were very pleased with ourselves!

I was sensible enough to realise that I just couldn't quit my current job – I needed it to fund the new business. So for a while I worked part time, started the business and was being a Mum to two children under two. It was difficult at times, but luckily Scott was there the whole time to support me.

It was just before Christmas in December 2008 that I decided I wasn't going back to work after the holidays. It was stressing me out too much and the new business was just starting to get a few clients. I had a "gut" feeling that I'd be fine.

That Christmas we went and visited my parents who lived over 1600km away. I had to take my laptop and all my paperwork with me as two of my new clients wanted me to work during the Christmas break. This meant I missed out on a lot of outings etc with my family, but in my mind I had to make sacrifices in order to make my business successful. (Thank goodness I know better now!)

Mid - January of 2008 was terrible. Most of my clients finally took time off which meant I had no work to do so, no income. I began wondering if I had done the right thing. Was I cut out to do this? Was I being unrealistic?

It got to a stage where I decided that I was going to have to learn transcription. I had another VA who was willing to train me and hire me once I had my skills up.

Well it all seemed like a good idea at the time, but after 5 minutes I was bored. I did put 100% effort in and even bought a good quality headset and pedal! But alas it wasn't meant to be. I take my hat off to anyone who does transcription!

But things have a funny way of turning out. The day after my transcription disaster I got three brand new clients! And I can honestly say, since that day I haven't had a day where I think "oh, where is the next client coming from?!"

Around March/April of 2009 I had to deal with sacking my first client. This was one of the hardest and scariest things I ever had to do. The client had begun to expect me to be at their beck and call 24 hours a day 7 days a week. I was NOWHERE NEAR being paid enough to deal with that. They began to get abusive and quite nasty so I had to make a decision. Keep them and deal with the problem OR let them go and wait for the next new client to come along?

In the end I made the decision to let them go. I couldn't get her to see reason and the whole situation was getting way too stressful. As you can imagine, they weren't very happy but it was a clean break and I felt as though a weight had been lifted – I had my life back!

By June 2009 I was working almost full time in the business. Scott had a full time job so we rarely got to see each other and our children were in day-care almost 5 days a week. This wasn't the way we wanted it to be.

Things had to change....

So on June 30, 2009, Scott quit his fulltime job and joined me in the business as a partner. It was a risky move, we had a family and a mortgage, but we both knew we could do it. Scott was going to work in the business 2-3 days a week and be a stay at home dad on the other days.

Funnily enough, a week after Scott left his job, he was offered a casual job at one of the local businesses which he accepted. This was our "fallback" in case anything went wrong. The job only involved 3 shifts a month so our plans weren't disrupted.

During this time, the business started to grow without us really realising it. I mean we knew we had more and more work coming in, but we didn't really realise how much. It got to a point where I was working almost 7 days a week. Again, this was never the intention of the business so something had to be done...

When I first started Typengraphics, I read about Multi VA businesses. I thought wow, how cool would it be to have your own team of Virtual Assistants? I didn't think it would ever happen to my little home business, although deep down I'm sure part of me did actually want to get to that point.

So, when the work starting becoming overwhelming I decided to hire a sub contractor. Now being the control freak that I am, this was a very hard decision for me to make. Even though I only had one person working with me it was still a daunting prospect. But in order for the business to grow I had to step out of my comfort zone and face my fears head on. Boy what a difference that made! It was great having someone by my side to help me.

It was around this time I began having problems with another of my clients. Things just weren't going as smoothly as they should. Although I had spoken to them about my concerns, they assured me everything was ok, but I just couldn't shake that feeling. However, for now I decided to leave things how they were and put it in the "too hard" basket.

The business continued to grow and grow. By this time I was becoming more and more interested in website design and development. Ironically, when I started the business that was one thing I SWORE I'd never do – but as the saying goes "never say never". I had also been given a great opportunity to be mentored by someone who I had admired from afar. This person had seen a design I had done for my own business and wanted something similar for theirs. I felt honoured that someone actually sat up and took notice of something that I had done. It was a real first for me. Although the mentoring no longer continues, I truly treasure the lessons that I learnt.

By June 2010 Typengraphics was keeping both Scott and myself busy. We had a team of 10 subcontractors and we soon had to start a waiting list for clients. Things were going great…until I learnt that you should always follow up on what your sub contractors are doing.

Over a period of about 5 months, I had two subcontractors go AWOL, three totally mucked up client jobs (even after being briefed a number of times), and another closed their business. Everything was a horrid mess. I had people ringing me left, right and centre wanting to know what was happening. It was at that point that I was ready to shut everything down. I'd had enough and didn't want to deal with this "crap" anymore.

But, that little fire inside me wouldn't die. After a day or so of feeling sorry for myself, I took stock and cleaned up the mess. Things are never as bad as they first seemed. I calmed everyone down and worked through all the problems. It was a lesson I'll never forget. In the rush to keep up with the workload I'd neglected to follow up on things, which is a HUGE 'no no'. Now I work with a small team whom I know that I can rely on and trust. I won't hire just anyone off the street ever again!

I also decided to let go of my second client. The situation with the client whom I mentioned earlier hadn't improved – in fact it was getting worse. Again, once I had let them go, I felt that a weight had been lifted from my shoulders. I knew I had made the right decision.

This gave me time to sit and have a good hard look at the business. It was then I realised that I had found my Niche clients without even trying! Ninety percent of our clients come from referrals, so naturally they all tend to be in the same industry, which in my case is Internet Marketers. Somehow this had slipped by unnoticed, but I realised it was something I had to capitalise on. I began increasing the services of the business to include teleseminar assistance, Wordpress sales pages, online business management – all things that assisted an Internet Marketer with their day to day business. Then things just went wild!

I started getting emails and calls about our services – we had become known as "a one stop shop" for internet marketers! I truly wish I could say that I sat down and mapped this out to make it happen, but I didn't.

I believe that our company's strong work ethic and high level of customer service puts us in front of our competitors. We make a promise to our clients that we won't run out on them or do them out of $1000s of dollars. Many of them have been burnt by other businesses in the past so by the time they get to us, they are concerned that we are just another "fly by nighter" (and rightly so!). We work hard to make sure that they know we are in it for the long haul!

Recently we decided to split Typengraphics. Scott has been handling all our graphic design and print work which has just exploded in the last 3 months and we feel that the name Typengraphics just doesn't really fit with the nature of what I do. So, we have just started our second business called "Backstage Helper" which will assist Internet Marketers/Coaches with their online business. We will also be launching Backstage Director which will be one on one coaching for clients who prefer to do the work themselves but would like some one on one coaching.

If someone had said to me "Tania, in two years time you will be running two successful businesses from home" I would have laughed and laughed. Why? Because I didn't believe I could do it.

Now, however, I believe that if you have a burning passion for what you do, have that fire burning brightly in your belly, and you can feel your face light up every time you talk about your business you WILL be successful.

It's only when passion is gone, that fire begins to dwindle and your face is expressionless, that your business will be unsuccessful.

I have been fortunate enough to have met the most amazing and influential people along this journey - all who have helped me in their own way with my business. I have an amazing new mentor (whom I've cried to when it all gets too hard). I have also met people who want to work with me on joint ventures, have me speak at their events, on their tele-seminars/webinars – it sometimes still seems a little surreal.

The future holds some great new adventures. My next goal is to spend a lot more time with my family while still running our successful businesses.

I KNOW it can be done and I WILL achieve it!

If you are thinking about starting or restructuring your business use my checklist to see if you are ready…

1. Got the passion?

2. Got the fire?

Then Go For It!

Written by: *Tania Smith*
www.typengraphics.com.au

Chapter 12 - Trusted Advisors
By: John A J McCann

Background
I began my career in 1965 in a large corporation in Sydney, Australia. I worked in IT as a programmer, analyst, project leader, chief information officer and finally I ran my own IT Company until 1988.

Then in 1989, after 24 years in IT, a board room coup resulted in separation from my career, my assets and a wonderful IBM dealership. A supreme court judge found in our favour but nevertheless we elected not to spend 2 years in litigation and decided to get on with our lives and a whole new direction.

Following is a brief account of the establishment of OrgPsych and the Helper Agent ® family around Australia.

In 1990 at the age of 46 it was difficult to obtain work in IT so I joined a Real Estate office, the Professionals in Berowra in Sydney Australia, as an agent with no previous experience.

Right from the start I was successful. I realised that I didn't need to be 'hard nosed' and pushy. I could be a consultative style of agent which was my natural style. I also quickly realised that agents did not sell property, people bought houses. The real selling occurred when getting the listing. To be successful I needed to be a good lister and I had to sell myself to get the listing. Therefore I needed to be nice and friendly so people would like me and list with me.

In 1992 I was head hunted and joined the leading national and international Real Estate Group, Jones Lang Wootton [LaSalle], responsible for Commercial sales in the Sydney city fringe region.

Then in 1994 we had a 'sea change' when we moved to Port Macquarie (400 kms north of Sydney). I joined Raine & Horne and was their top producer for 5 years.

Reflection
In 1996 reflecting on my life as a real estate agent I was amazed at the personal & poignant stories people were sharing with me. Some of the memorable ones include, a family who had two children, one of whom was killed in a car accident and their other child was killed on their way home to attend the funeral. The heart break was incredible. Many times mothers would share with me the pain of losing a child from suicide because of drug addiction.

In many instances I never knew what to say to help them so I just listened. The more I listened and showed genuine interest in people the more they told me. Also, I began giving away a wonderful book Feel the Fear and Do It Anyway by Susan Jeffers. I did this because I wanted to help these people who were struggling. The book was recommended by a psychologist when I was struggling, so I thought, well this may just help them.

The experience of listening to stories of loss, sadness, grief and pain generated a desire in me to do more. This together with a desire to help people be the best they could, prompted me to study psychology so I could understand more about human behaviour and people's thoughts and feelings.

Concurrently I established a consultancy known as OrgPsych. The company specialises in improving individual effectiveness. We work with real estate agents helping them to improve performance by teaching relationship building skills, and negotiation techniques. We coach and mentor both agents and principals. Our work is based on peer reviewed research and practical experience.

Deep life changing reflection
In 2002 I sat down with pen and exercise book (journal) and began to think more deeply and write about my life as a real estate agent. I had been successful but what exactly was it I was doing to achieve that success? I wanted to become clear on exactly what it was so I could better help other real estate agents.

What are we really doing as agents? What do we think and feel? What impact do we have? What are people who use our services feeling and doing? What do people think of agents? What affects an agent's performance? What was I doing when in a person's home listing the property for sale? Following are some of the reflections, insights and learnings.

As real estate agents we have a significant responsibility. Most of the time when we are appointed to sell a home we are dealing with a person or family's entire wealth. As agents we are in a unique position. Our modern world has become one dominated by high security, increased vigilance and a high tech society which fosters reduced personal contact. Agents are one of the few professions who go into people's houses on a regular basis including when they are not there – solicitors don't, bank staff don't, and doctors don't any more. We as agents are asked to share people's private space – their personal private world – usually reserved for family and friends. What an honour and a privilege.

As I documented my listing presentations to try and understand the components and teach them to new sales agents, the word empathy hit me. According to Gerard Egan (2) the techniques for establishing a therapeutic relationship using empathic listening were the same as those for obtaining a trusting relationship and winning business with a client in any professional service firm. Unknowingly I had been using these powerful communication skills as a real estate agent.

The more I reflected, the more I realised an agent's performance is impacted by a number of psychological factors. Issues such as self-esteem, self-confidence, self-efficacy, trust, respect, values, fear, anxiety, rejection, thinking, behaviour, moods, feelings, goals, relationships, motivation, self-awareness, personality, and more. Of critical importance is what mind set (paradigm) the agent has. What's in his or her heart when thinking about their clients? How do they feel about their clients? What meaning do they attribute to what they are doing?

With the help of an experienced trainer and wonderful friend Pippa Furey we developed a program to help agents be more self-aware, to clarify values such as empathy, integrity, respect, genuineness and to teach agents to listen empathically.

Selling one's home is an emotional and stressful experience for most people. I remember an elderly lady who had just lost her husband and the loving relationship of 67 years and was moving into a retirement village;

probably her last move. Emotions of grief, sadness and even hopelessness from a combination of losses.

Then there have been the times when a family breadwinner has been transferred, the family will be leaving friends and relatives, facing separation, whether it be temporary or permanent.   Emotions include excitement, sadness, anxiety and apprehension.

As an estate agent you might have been contracted to sell a house but it is also a home. Often what clients want from their agents is not just a good sale but just as importantly, understanding of what they are experiencing. Help not just with the physical aspects of moving but just as importantly, understanding in coping with the more invasive psychological issues which typically accompany relocation. Increased levels of feelings such as fear, anxiety, grief, excitement, uncertainty and impatience to name just a few.

I recall reflecting on how highly regarded nurses are compared to real estate agents. In surveys on people most trusted reported in the media, nurses and volunteer fire fighters are the most trusted and car salesmen and real estate agents the least. Why, I thought, can't agents be helpers just like nurses, psychologists and social workers? Thus was born the term Helper Agent ®.

As my journey continues. I have had to get to know myself better (increase my self-awareness)! Who am I? What do I want to do with the rest of my life? What's my purpose? (what's it all about Alfie?)?

The Journey – Insights, Learning, Suggestions
In the second part of this chapter I want to share with you a brief insight into some of my epiphanies, paradigm shifts,

insights and learning in this incredible journey. I hope that they add value to your journey in some way.

The power of Self-Awareness
Who am I? What am I about? And why is this important?
Gaining a better understanding of yourself and why you think, feel and act the way you do, will help you be more objective in understanding other people's feelings, thinking and behaviour. Self-aware people will have a competitive advantage in business in the coming decade.

The Renaissance is regarded as a bridge between the middle ages and the modern era. Renaissance (Italian: "Rinascimento" be born again) (3). In some ways I experienced a mini 'renaissance' - a shift from 'left' brain to 'right' brain. A shift from a focus on the logical and tasks to embracing the human dynamic with all its complexities. A world that was heart and people oriented; the world of literacy, poetry, psychology, philosophy, sociology and eastern philosophies of the Tao, Chan (Zen) Buddhism, meditation and yoga.

Methods of increasing Self-Awareness
Self-awareness can be increased by self reflection and writing these reflections especially with a pen in hand (23); by moments of insight; from feedback from others and by completion of psychological instruments and assessment tools such as MBTI (4) and Genos Emotional Intelligence (5).

Reflection - self-awareness – self development
"The quality of our reflection is the underlying driver of our performance improvement" (6).

When I was in transition from a 25 year career in IT to a career as a real estate agent and then on to a career in psychology, reflection has helped me identify what I wanted to do for the rest of my life.

The more I learned about the human condition and how to change behaviour the more I have realised the power of written reflection. Socrates was so right "The unexamined life is not worth living!"(3). Research is demonstrating that journaling using the right questions is a powerful way to change how we think, feel and act (7).

The questions we ask determine our world. Some powerful questions you could ask yourself are: What's life trying to teach me? What benefit can I find in this adverse situation? Is this the person I really want to be? What's right about my current circumstances? (8).

What do I want to do for the rest of my life – in a sentence, help people not die with their music locked inside!

Values in Action
So what are some of the values, behaviours and attitudes of a helper?

What is a helping relationship? One of the best ways to characterise a helping relationship is through the values that should permeate and drive it. Values are not just ideals. They are also a set of practical criteria for making decisions and they are key drivers of behaviour.

Principle-centred Values and practices
Business research studies into long term business success show that integrity, empathy, ethical behaviour, building trusting relationships, servant leadership, being socially responsible and having a mission of wanting to make the world a better place are behind the outstanding

performance of companies like Commerce Bank, South West Airlines, Google, Toyota etc , (9 and 10).

Conducting business is, in essence, establishing an interpersonal relationship. The ideal business relationship when negotiating with customers and clients is a working alliance (11) which builds trust where you, the expert, become a trusted advisor.

Empathy
Empathy is essentially being able to 'emotionally exchange places with others', 'take their point of view', 'care for them' and 'consider them to be at least equal and at times more important than you'. Ego-driven arrogance or selfishness can play no part in exercising empathy.

Integrity
Integrity is character – the personal values and ethics that ground your behaviour in moral principles. "Do unto others….." Integrity is the quality that assures people can be trusted, they will be honest, and they will do as they say. If people trust them with confidential information people know they will not disclose it to others. Finally if you make a commitment you will follow through on it.

The How.
I will achieve the 'what' by having and setting goals, by learning, by being positive, self-disciplined, and persistent and by building breakthrough relationships.

Set goals
What is it that you want to achieve (an outcome goal) and how will you achieve it (a process goal)?
In 1996 during my initial year of psychological study I wrote an outline of my future personal and professional life. This outline contained who I really wanted to be and with whom I wished to share it (my amazing supportive and loving

wife). My vision was that I'd be a psychologist helping people in business. It has all happened. I rewrote this outline many times. In 1996 I also had a simple plaque made up with my name and qualifications on it then in 2004 I graduated with those qualifications.

When studying psychology we were told that to become a psychologist we were required to achieve a 'Distinction' average to advance to Honours and then Masters. To help me achieve the goal of obtaining a distinction (which was very difficult) I wrote a "D" in the top corner of every page of each text book I read. Also on book marks which I still have, I wrote the inspirational words from W. Mitchell "If not you, Who?" "If not now, When?" and "If not here, Where?" (12). I used these quotes to inspire me to push on even when I felt overwhelmed and at times desperate when I was studying, working full time and often struggling personally

Become a student of life - Self Development
I see myself as a student of life, a curious child. I am a constant learner which I do through reading books, journals, conferences and formal study. My car is a mobile leaning centre. I have listened to Covey's 7 Habits of Highly effective people on cassette (showing my age) over and over again and now I listen to it on CD. Other material I have listened to over the years includes, Norman Vincent Peale, Dale Carnie, John Powell and many others. I also learn from my clients and students when I teach and coach; I love learning.

Learn to Fail or Fail to learn (16).
On his way to the presidency, Abraham Lincoln dropped out of grade school, went broke in a business, and took 15 years to repay his creditors. He ran for the House of Representatives twice and lost twice, and ran for the Senate twice, and lost twice. But Lincoln's failures are not what he is remembered for. Try to make a learning experience out of every failure. Every time we fail, we learn something. Look at failure as an opportunity to grow. Don't

dwell on our mistakes, profit from them. What is life trying to teach me here?

John P. Kotter, a Harvard Professor studied Harvard MBA graduates to find out how they were getting on 20 years after graduation (16). Most were successful however, a small number were extremely successful. Kotter discovered the two characteristics the very successful graduates had were (i) a passion for whatever they were doing and (ii) a thirst for learning with the humility to know they did not know it all.

Positivity
While reflecting, in this case thinking about events of the day with a pen and journal for example, I have a list of 10 positive emotions: joy, gratitude, serenity, interest, hope, pride, love, amusement, inspiration and awe in front of me (8). By reliving times when we experience these emotions and by focusing on their occurrence we are building psychological capacity. This will increase positivity which is an important factor as we strive to be the best we can be. This process of building positivity helps people flourish and become more resilient so they can bounce back from setbacks. We are not suggesting you get rid of negative emotion, we can't and we should not try to do so. The goal is to experience three times more positive emotions over time than negative emotions.

To monitor your positivity and become more self-aware, you can go to www.positivityratio.com and register. Take the test as often as you like (8).

Be Self Disciplined
"The harder we work, the luckier we get."(17)
Whilst studying psychology in my early fifties I was too tired to study at night so I got up early. For 9 years I would get up at around 4am, study until 7am then shower, have breakfast and go to work for the day. When I was admitted to the Masters program at Macquarie University in Sydney

I was working in Port Macquarie as a real estate agent. On Monday at 1 pm I would drive the 4.5 hours to Sydney to attend lectures until 9pm then at times go to a friend's office in Asquith and sleep on a swag. I'd get up at 4am shower and drive back to Port Macquarie, go to work as a real estate agent until 5pm.

Be Persistent

What separates successful people from the rest? The answer lies in what Winston Churchill said – "Never, never, never, never give in." Mental toughness is the ability to keep bouncing back to fight our way to the top – despite numerous setbacks. Persistence prevails when all else fails.

Emotions

We need to understand our emotions because "Emotions guide, enrich, and ennoble life; they provide meaning to everyday existence..........Emotions promote behaviours that protect life...and compel the termination of life" (22). All reality is personal and infused with affect (emotion).

Emotions have been the elephant in the living room waiting to be acknowledged by Business Academics, Corporate Executives and Economists.

Emotions are concrete, physiological states and they are contagious. Emotions are the result of changes in body states, changes in adrenalin flow, heart beat, blood pressure, galvanic skin responses, breathing (22). Emotions (feelings) pervade every aspect of our lives, our relationships with others and with our self. When we bottle up feelings we distort our thinking. Angry people arguing are invariably irrational.

Consumer behaviour research is showing that in product and service branding, right brain words e.g.: help, care, love are more effective in creating customer loyalty. Arousing consumer's emotion in positive ways generates loyalty.

Empathic Listening

If you want to interact effectively with me, to influence me – your spouse, your partner, your child, your neighbour, your boss, your co-worker, your friend, your client – you first need to understand me.

When we listen, we might hear, and it may be that we understand. But, if we do not communicate our listening in a way that lets the other person know we have heard them and truly understood them, empathy has not occurred. There is no connection, our hearts have not connected (18). Empathic listening is, having heard the words and sensed the emotion, we tell the other person what we heard and how we believe they are feeling.

For example, a potential client in her home says to me "John, Arthur can't look after the gardens like he used he's not well enough!" My response "You're worried Arthur might injure himself in the garden!" It doesn't matter if we don't get the emotion 'spot on' as long as we try. The person knows we care so we are doing our best to understand them and that communicates the most positive message of all (19).

Be "for" the client an I-Thou relationship (20).

This is the fundamental stance that one human being ought always to take toward another person, a relationship of respect in which the other individual is viewed as having intrinsic value, value in and of himself or herself, regardless of whether that individual can produce any further value for you (20).

A few last suggestions

Focus on what you really want to do and are good at – 'having a cause is a magnet for passion' (24);

Write down a mission and vision (purpose and values) on one page and generate outcome and process goals – what are my outcomes (income or helping people) and process goals (e.g. how will you achieve your goals).

Become a student of life with the curiosity of a child rummaging through a toy box!

Create business alliances with organisations with similar values – this is a largely untapped business development strategy;

Build your vision and mission around the philosophy of loyal clients (21).

Commit to more 'Face Time with Clients' to build trust (21);

Commit to continuous improvement so you become the best you can be.

Commit to daily reflection with the 10 positive emotions in view.

Conclusion

"We shall never cease from exploring, and at the end of our exploration will be to arrive at the beginning and know the place for the first time (25)." My personal motto is "love, learn and leave a legacy". I now see my journey as just that - a journey. I will only really understand my life's purpose which might be viewed as a patch-work quilt when the last piece of the puzzle - my passing this earthly life - is in place. I feel blessed that I have worked as a real estate agent because I learnt so much about people and life.

Acknowledgements:

Susan Patricia McCann without her love and support this would not have been possible; Sally Patricia Campling (nee McCann) whose help was invaluable; and Pippa Furey who believed in me and the project when I had doubts and gave so much of her time.

References

1.   Bruce Fairchild Barton (1886 – 1967),
       American Author, advertising executive and politician
2.   The Skilled Helper – Gerard Egan
3.   Wikipedia, the free encyclopaedia.

4. www.cpp.com
5. www.genosinternational.com
6. Msceit emotional intelligence seminar Sydney Australia, Paul Nesbit
7. Opening Up: The Healing Power of Expressing Emotions, James W. Pennebaker,
8. Positivity – Barbara Fredrickson.
9. Good to Great – Jim Collins
10. Firms of Endearment,
    Raj Sisodia, Jag Sheth and David B. Wolfe.
11. Getting to Yes – Roger Fisher & William Ury
12. W Mitchell, motivational speaker and businessman who suffered burns to 65% of his body and became paralysed from the waist down.
13. Samuel Goldwyn was born Schmuel Gelbfisz (1879–1974), American film producer.
14. Integrity - Henry Cloud
15. Difficult Conversations,
    Douglas Stone, Bruce Patton & Sheila Heen
16. I and Thou – Martin Buber
17. Clients for Life - Jagdish Sheth & Andrew Sobel.
18. Handbook of Emotions, 2nd edition.
    Michael Lewis, Jeanette M. Haviland-Jones.
19. The Other 90%. Robert K. Cooper.
20. If Aristotle Ran General Motors – Tom Morris
21. Thomas Stearns Elliot (1888–1965),
    American-born English poet, playwright and literary critic.

Further Reading

Feel the Fear and Do It Anyway – Susan Jeffers
The 7 Habits of Highly Effective People – Stephen Covey
The Trusted Advisor – David Maister, Charles Green & Robert Galford
The Power of Positive Thinking – Norman Vincent Peale
Counter Clockwise – Ellen Langer

Written by: John A J McCann

www.orgpsych.com.au and www.helperagent.com.au

Chapter 13 – An Opportunity Seized
By: Bill McPherson

My name is William (Bill) McPherson and as I write I'm enjoying my 85th Year on this earth.

I've had a most amazing life and the purpose of writing this is to pass on at least some of the experience in a few pages so I've chosen only one example of an amazing experience which presented itself, without my instigation. And what can happen if you grab opportunity, instead of letting it go by.

The story involves my friend, Charles. Charles was an architect who worked for a firm and had a burning desire to create something of significance to launch him into private practice and give recognition of his creative ability.

Charles had a magnificent house in a significant street very close to the heart of Melbourne which contained a small suite of offices that he had leased to me for a development project in which I was involved with a small staff of three.

We became firm friends as Charles watched my project develop and he became most interested.

Charles was a great big handsome man and his accent was most becoming to the ladies - we had nicknamed him 'The Count'

His shoulders were so broad, that when we buried him some years later, the mourners had to move away while the cemetery staff dug a wider hole to accommodate his coffin!

One day Charles said to me 'Bill, you must come with me to see Sir Roger'. Now I didn't know of or know any Sir

Roger so I asked how I could help my friend and what was it all about?

It turned out that Charles had developed a design for a factory produced transportable home, a concept that to date had not really been successful in the housing market.

Charles had become friendly with Sir Roger as a result of his daily walk to work. Regularly Sir Roger would drive past and offer him a lift so they had 15 minutes each time to chat about whatever. Charles had told him of the project so Sir Roger invited him to show him the designs to see if he could help. Hence the request for me to go and help present the concept as Charles recognized his language difficulty and felt I could present the details more clearly.

So I studied the drawings and thought they had merit. The concept used a truss wall such as was used to span openings like river crossings and would be rigid enough for transportation from factory to site so I thought it was a good idea.

I still had no inkling of who Sir Roger was but agreed to be present to support my friend

We duly arrived at the meeting to discover Sir Roger was a Director of several larger companies and was most highly respected in the commercial field.

He listened carefully to my presentation and congratulated Charles on the work he had done. He then picked up the phone and called an associate in Sydney and I heard him say 'Alan, I think I have something here you would like to see'

Suddenly Charles and I found we had plane tickets presented to us for the next day and we flew up to Sydney to meet 'Alan', the MD of a large aluminium fabrication plant. He listened to our story, obviously impressed by the introduction and implied support of 'Sir Roger'.

'Alan' then showed us the reason for the interest shown by them both.

In the yard they had a large container from their American associates loaded with aluminium insulated panels. They had no idea what to do with them and quickly saw them as Sir Roger had, to be suitable for the cladding of homes using Charles' designs.

That afternoon Alan put together a team of draftsmen under Charles direction to develop a series of plans to present to an acquaintance in Canberra and suggested I leave Charles with them and come back in a week prepared to take the presentation to Canberra.

When I returned the package was ready and an appointment had been made. Alan took us to a building he had just bought on the 'Rocks' and indicated an office suite that would be for Charles and his project – all this happening at lightning speed.

Do remember this was in the 60's when Canberra was exploding.

Alan's contact turned out to be the Chief of the Housing Department who loved the concept and who obviously had great respect for Sir Roger and Alan. He took me aside and told me that all of the builders in Canberra had got so far behind the number of arrivals in Canberra that he needed help with homes, now!.

He then suggested he could give me an order today for $1,000,000 if that could start us off. He had also arranged for his counterpart in Melbourne to be present to meet with us.

We had arranged lunch for the group at the hotel on the lake and in a joyous mood enjoyed partaking of some of the beverages as a sign of our success.

Over lunch our contact told us he had just one small act to cover – previously a wall panel construction had emitted toxic smoke during a fire and he had agreed the fire chief could have approval of any such project so he had made a appointment to take us to the fire Chief after our lunch. Once the Fire Chief's approval had been obtained he would give us the order to take back to Sydney.

On arrival at our appointment with the Fire Chief, we who had enjoyed lunch were all bright and breezy, still elated by our success. The Chief was not in the same mood.

We had with us a small section of the panel for demonstration and the Chief stood it against a wall and produced from a cabinet the biggest blow lamp I had ever seen – I swear it had at least a 2" nozzle!

So he fired it up while we all watched and stood it close to the panel.

In seconds the panel front disintegrated and toxic white smoke filled the room.

'Sorry' said the Chief – if you can bring me one that doesn't do that I'm happy to give you approval.

Of course we were defeated and came home to lick our wounds.

Our lesson was that given the right contacts at the right time mountains can be climbed. Our passion and enthusiasm, our belief that people were willing to help, had carried us to the brink.

Charles and I remained firm friends. After about 5 years of development my project didn't develop legs and without further funding it had to be disbanded after a non affordable loss.

Charles then bought me a loss making restaurant which I turned into a total of three and left the industry after 10 good years. It was in that period that we lost Charles – I guess that's another story

What's the moral of this one – people are waiting to help you if the idea is good enough – do not be afraid – they respect ideas, enthusiasm – action – and don't forget to smile!

Written by: *Bill McPherson*

www.AroundAltona.com.au

Chapter 14 – From Scientist to Naturopath
By: Doreen Schwegler

End of High School: Decisions.
Step back into 1978, end of HSC exams. 17 year old me was having a tough time deciding whether to become a Physical Education teacher, a laboratory scientist or to just study Science at Melbourne Uni. The lure of overseas travel opportunities, an actual career at the end of my course and a picture of myself in a white lab coat peering down a microscope won me over to choosing to study at RMIT in an Applied Science Degree in Laboratory Science.

First Career, Travel & a New Direction.
Several years later, having had graduated and worked in laboratories in Melbourne and England, I was travelling on an extensive overseas trip and was in China. Two events there changed my destiny. I had seen various shops in Hong Kong and China with exotic looking herbs, antlers, and potions. I had a nasty cough and visited a pharmacy type shop. Despite my limited Chinese (I could say hello, thank-you and count to ten), and the assistant not speaking any English, I managed to communicate my problem (by coughing). I was given some pills with a picture of an obscure fruit on the bottle, instructed with hand gesticulations as to how to take them. They seemed to work fairly efficiently. At the same time there was a person at the hostel who knew someone from Melbourne that was doing a course at the Southern School of Naturopathy. I had been brought up in an open minded family that used chiropractors for injuries and asthma, osteopaths for my turned eye as a child, and chamomile tea for upset tummies and the like. So the seed was planted to investigate a course in Natural Therapies.

Tip #1: Be on the lookout for opportunities and synchronicity.

Qualification #2 & the Pitfalls of Misinformation

On my return I applied and was accepted for the then 4 year Diploma of Applied Science in Naturopathy. I had anticipated doing the course for one year and seeing how it went. But my thirst for knowledge about natural treatments, and subjects including Psychology, Nutrition, and Herbal Medicine allowed no turning back. I graduated 4 years later in 1989. Part of our course in final year involved business studies, and we had to write a business plan. I did then, and still do have troubles anticipating costs, income and outcomes, but I ended up turning a spare bedroom in the house into a treatment room and hoped for the best.

Part of our training involved massage, and I studied further to complete a diploma. People who saw me for massage could then claim on some of the more enlightened private health insurance funds, and I could become a member of an association (now called AAMT) that did a group advertisement in the Yellow Pages. This gave some credibility to my services (there were still many confused people out there about what services exactly a "masseuse" actually did)!

Tip #2: Join an association to reap the benefits of group ads in yellow pages and to give credibility.

I made the mistake of placing an ad in the local paper. Did I have some strange phone calls (e.g. Do you do any "extras" etc)? I was rather naïve at first, but became quite adept at screening calls from men! I also wore a white coat that gave me an air of professionalism (at least I hoped). At the time I was fostering a dog (a fat Labrador called Kira who was very protective of me).I called her in on the odd occasion to check out some of the dubious clients. One particular memory is of a huge African with a crew cut knocked at my door for a "massage" appointment. After he came in (and saw the white coat, form to fill in with his personal details etc.), he politely asked if he could pop off to get some money from the Automatic teller. I quickly rang my next door neighbour in to hang around just in case. Needless to say he never returned!

Building a Business and a "New" Frontier:
Naturopathy was still in many people's minds a fish-slapping pseudo-profession. Most people were familiar with massage, but it took some convincing for clients to consider working with diet, herbs, nutritional supplements and herbs to help their health issues. But gradually my practice began to grow, and the acceptance of Naturopathy as a respectable profession. Initially my main source of clients was from word-of-mouth referrals and the group adverts under suburb name in yellow pages under ANTA (Australian Association of Natural Therapists). **(See Tip #2)** Networking at places like my local squash club, chatting with anyone that would listen (even my accountant), and my enthusiasm and belief about helping people also helped. I was still working part-time at pathology labs to pay the bills and receive a reliable income.

Tip #3: When starting a new venture, have a steady income stream as it usually takes a while to earn enough money to give up the "day job". Add a lot of start up expenses like joining associations, dispensary costs, marketing, insurance, utilities etc and it takes a while to reach "break even" let alone any profit.

Spanner in the works – marriage and babies!
Mr. Right comes into the picture, and 2 years later there was baby #1. Gorgeous, but time consuming! Between nappies (I do admit to having Nappy Wash service until she was toilet trained as I loathed disposables), breastfeeds (sometimes while seeing "old" clients that were OK with this), and many nocturnal sleep interruptions, I managed to resume seeing clients fairly quickly. Actually the **day after** I came home from hospital, the locum I'd organized for a patient didn't show up. Fortunately a friend

134

dropped in at the same time as the client (thanks Phil!), so I ended up seeing them and after finishing, seeing them both asleep – Emma on Phil's chest! I have been accused of being a workaholic (rightly so, no doubt), but this took the cake!

Tip #4. If you have babies, organize someone to look after your clients while you are on leave. When you return, set limits as to when you will see clients (preferably when partner is at home or someone can mind the offspring) and when you will answer the phone – especially if you are home based and your child is a poor sleeper! An **answering service is** essential.

There is some strange, natural reaction from clients that once you have your baby you have gone to some cyberspace land of parenthood, never to return!

Tip #5: Clarify to clients WHEN you anticipate returning - you can always change this should the circumstances change, so they DO know you are returning.

Internet wasn't accessible to ordinary people in those days (where I would have had everyone's email addresses and keep in touch at the click of a button). I certainly didn't have the time to write or call all my old clients (it's unbelievable how much time a little critter can zap out of your day), so it took a while for old clients to return and new clients to fill the gaps....

Space Invaders: Kids
Space was a challenging issue in our 10 square home. The baby's room doubled as a treatment room by day (baby moved into the lounge room, and it was closed off by a screen to avoid the clutter and mess one tiny tacker (and parent's) generate). She could then have her space back at night!

Tip#6: Always have professional looking spaces for clients.

Patients don't want to walk over toys and washing when they're seeing you for stress related issues or want a relaxing massage!

Baby #2 saw an even tighter fit in our house (nappy changes were in the laundry on top of the dishwasher). Opportunity knocked, and we built a purpose built house/clinic one street away on a corner allotment where the clinic entrance was separate and professional looking. This gave room for expansion, as there were 2 treatment rooms, and I could only work so many hours in the week, and wanted quality time with my kids and be able to take them to kinder, playgroup etc.

Expansion

I have tried many multilevel marketing schemes in my time – Bessemer ware as a teenager (I fell in love with the pots, pans and veggie chopper), Amway (I wanted to get the washing powder at cost), Go chi (I was harassed too many times by a colleague before I succumbed), Nikken (I liked the water filters) etc – all with the promise of fame and glory. One of the REALLY useful side-effects of these "fads" was the reading material they recommended, and that I read. One of the books talked about if you are self-employed, your income is limited by the amount of hours you work, or products you sell if that's the way you earn your money. What entrepreneurs do is to make money from others working for them, or investing in something that generates money regardless of whether they work or not!

Tip #7: Read LOTS of material not just about what you do, but HOW you do things and about how businesses run. I've listed some books at the end of this book that have influenced me in business and life.

A light bulb went off for me! This resulted in me renting the spare room initially to a psychologist. This involved issues with council to allow an extra practitioner to use the space. Some assistance from a helpful Town Planner, attendance at a council meeting, negotiations and payments eventually overcame that hurdle!

Tip #8: get quality advisors – accountants, town planners, business coaches as required.

Later my practice became so busy, I approached another excellent naturopath (who had a child in the same school as mine) to work a day a week in my practice. This turned into 2 then 3 days then full time. I got to be less stressed (for the time being), able to focus on the area I later specialized in (Natural Fertility), have new patients that were happier as they did not have to wait months to get an appointment to see me, and get a percentage of her fees! I also got in a massage therapist and subsequently another Naturopath that I could delegate to, so I was only working 50 hours a week (doing paperwork, attending professional education, unpacking boxes, seeing clients, networking and working ON the business).

Big Shifts in Thinking:

#1: Delegation
Things were looking good – I had a reliable client base and was actually banking money at the end of the day. But I was breathless answering phones, booking appointments, mixing herbs and trying to stay calm and focused seeing clients! One of the best advise was "why do a $15 (then) an hour job (e.g. answering phones, manage bookings etc) when you can pay someone to do this and earn $80 (then) an hour?" Whether to hire staff was one of the hardest, and in retrospect, one of the best decisions I ever made! I could see perhaps 2 more patients a day in the time I was spending doing the $15 an hour job that would easily pay for a helper. I misguidedly wondered how such a helper

could keep busy all day. How wrong could I have been! Not only did the one day a week quickly turn into 5 days a week and 2 evenings, but patients were happier (they had my undivided attention), I was less stressed, had herbs made up for me, products unpacked and put away, and twice a week I even had the meal cooked, washing put out on the line and the dishwasher loaded, washed and emptied. Initially my helper was a "Jack of all Trades", but this streamlined into a cleaning lady who irons and cooks, and admin lady.

Tip #9: Be very clear about your expectations and job description before hiring. A receptionist or office administrator does not want to cook or clean if they aren't expected to, but may be happy to help out in the initial stages if they know it is only temporary and they are not being taken advantage of!

#2 Weight Loss:
One of the biggest issues I had with clients was helping them lose weight. I would give someone a clear diet plan and careful instructions, only to see them months later at the supermarket 2 sizes larger and not to happy. Enter an influential client (let's call her Jo). She came to me asking about buying sachets for a new weight loss program from a Naturopath in Melton called Tony le Vannais. It involved 3 meals a day that the client prepared themselves, and a small milk type flavoured drink they had in between meals. I contacted Tony (as we knew each other), and eventually took on a franchise-type arrangement for the Essendon/Moonee Ponds area. This impacted my sales and client base in leaps and bounds! It is a smaller part of my practice now as there is a lot of competition out there (as well as I am not focusing as much energy as I could, but delegating to my colleague I work with), but it certainly was busy in the initial phases!

Tip #10: Watch trends; go for something that has been recommended and tried, that meets a need in your niche or in the community.

The Big Move

My teenage daughter (my noisy conscience), complained constantly about many things related to me working from home. This included:

- the invasion of her privacy
- her inability to comfortably invite friends over (without being told to "turn down the TV" or "Don't make so much noise")
- having to share the kitchen table with "randoms" like a receptionist having lunch or the family computer with the bookkeeper)
- the lack of me "being there" emotionally (I was always slipping into my office to finish the days reconciliation or to call a client etc).
- Phone calls accidentally answered from the business line from the cordless phone
- Having clients ring the doorbell to collect products out-of-hours
- And the list goes on

As her VCE was fast approaching, I had regular meetings with business coach and mentor, Andrea Henricksen, about the prospects of moving my clinic. The 2 rooms at home were being fully utilized most days, and I wanted to expand the services I could provide. We worked (and are still working on) a business plan, and estimated the financial implications of me moving out from home. I found an ideal location nearby home with 3 treatment rooms, a large area for off street parking and a garage that could be converted to a yoga and personal training studio.

The Successful Business Now:

"All Degrees of Health" is a now a one stop wellness shop that has a wonderful team of highly motivated and effective professionals:

- Acupuncturist and Doctor of Chinese Medicine, Robert Gentile who has post-graduate qualifications in gynecology and fertility treatments and is knowledgeable, approachable and highly talented at what he does
- Osteopath Trent Danaher who helps with pain and injury and has magic hands
- Psychologist Oriella Cattapan who deals with the emotional side of disease
- Remedial Massage Therapist – Susanne Debono who uses massage and Emmett technique to sooth muscles, ease pain and balance bodies
- Reflexologist Maria Vella who also does an amazingly relaxing Hot Rock Massage
- Spiritual Healer and crystal therapist Rose Gentile who has helped clear the energy blocks from my clients, staff and myself to move on in life
- Shiatsu therapist Ruk De Silva who balances meridians, bodies and minds with her healing hands
- Naturopath Rosie Khayat who specializes in Weight loss and women's health, and is enthusiastic and competent.
- Learning Therapists Christine Manetta and Lorraine Callega who help children with learning and auditory processing problems and help happy families
- Associated practitioners: Personal Trainer, yoga classes, Business coach and hypnotherapist.

We also run monthly educational workshops covering many topics from Effective Weight Loss to Optimizing health through Genetic Testing!

Enter my passion: Healthy Babies!
I specialize in Natural Fertility Management. This involves helping couples overcome delays in getting pregnant, dealing with recurrent miscarriages, helping prepare for a healthy pregnancy or supporting assisted reproductive techniques (like IVF). I have a scrapbook album and photo board full of pictures of healthy babies, sometimes conceived after unsuccessful attempts at IVF, much angst, money and medication. One of my clients contacted the "Herald-Sun" about my work and I had an article written about my work. This and subsequent articles in the media, a Current Affair interview, website presence and word-of-mouth referrals from happy customers and their families keep me busy in this very rewarding field.

Other Words of Wisdom:
Tip # 11: Keep your website up-to-date., and consider a u-tube clip as people love visuals

Tip # 12: Keep a reliable data base with email addresses to keep in regular contact with clients. Your current clients know who you are but can forget you exist.

Tip # 13: Education is critical – clients may not realize that an osteopath can help with headaches, not just back problems. Or that acupuncture can assist with hormone regulation.

Tip # 14: Keep the customers happy. Be flexible, supportive and available. It is 50 times cheaper to look after a current client than to get a new client through advertising etc. Workshops, educational emails, handouts etc are invaluable.

Tip # 15: Effective communication with staff and practitioners - Regular staff meetings, emails, get togethers so we all know what each other does and be comfortable cross referring.

Future Plans:
Educational Programs:
- First Aid
- Birth Education Classes
- Reflexology and Massage
- Gift making using natural products e.g. Scrubs, face creams etc.

Our monthly brainstorming sessions will think of some more ideas!

Recommended Reading:
1. Rich Dad Poor Dad
2. The 4 hour Work Week
3. Work harder Not Smarter
4. Paper Flow
5. Organizing form the Inside Out
6. A is for Attitude
7. The Business of Healing
8. Regular Marketing emails from crocodile marketing or similar
9. The Power of Now

Epilogue:
My daughter finished Year 12 in peace and quiet. She still finds things to complain about, but appreciates that "randoms" no longer invade her space. She makes full use of most of the practitioners a short walk from our home. My son is happy that he can play uninterrupted on his Wii without worrying about volume control! I come home and wonder what there is to do – for about a millisecond- then I see the washing, cooking, cleaning, notes from school...

Written By : Doreen Schwegler

www.alldegreesofhealth.com.au

About the Contributors

Brenda Thomson

Brenda is the CEO of Networking World, an online directory of business networking resources for small business owners. She provides training in business networking and strategic alliances for small business owners and entrepreneurs. Networking World also provides a range of online and offline networking opportunities. Brenda is one of the instigators behind the **"SMART People SMART Business"** book idea, which is just one example of the WIN WIN strategic alliance opportunities that Brenda is passionate about helping small business owners to identify and create.

Brenda can be contacted at Networking World www.networkingworld.net.au. By phone on 1300 790 997 by email at Brenda@networkingworld.net.au or by visiting her BLOG www.theSMARTBusinessNetworker.com

Karen Glass

Karen Glass is a Professional Administration Consultant who works with small to medium enterprises to provide Executive Project and Office Management Services. By working with Time Well Spent business owners will be able to work collectively on developing successful business and marketing strategies as well as gaining their time back to grow their business. She partners with these companies to ensure they have more time to work ON their business rather than IN their business.

Dedicated, knowledgeable and experienced, working with Karen will mean that your **time is well spent**.

For more information please visit:
www.timewellspent.com.au

Marilyn Martyn

Originally Marilyn trained as a teacher and librarian specialising in children's literature. Her teaching experience has been in primary, secondary and independent schools.

Her career developed around her love of books, reading and teaching.

Marilyn has worked as a publisher's consultant in educational materials and marketing general books to bookstores. Her experience as a tutor for the National Evenstart Program, laid the foundations for her tutoring business which is now both online and offline.

Her website, www.superlearner.com.au has been developed as a way for her to share her knowledge and experience to enhance the online educational experience of as many people as possible.

You can contact Marilyn on her website or by email at support@superlearner.com.au

Fred Gillen

The SMART brain behind the SMART People SMART Business book series.

Fred is CEO of Nitty Gritty Business and an IT consultant with over 25 years experience assisting businesses gain the most value from their IT systems. He is a published author, keynote speaker, specialist trainer and Internet junkie. He has also created numerous on-line training videos to assist newbies get stared in Internet Marketing. Fred has made a number of these available at no charge so that even those on a limited budget can learn how Internet Marketing can assist their business. One of his latest additions can be found at www.Page1ofGoogle.com.

You can drop Fred an email at fred@fredgillen.com

Allen Suss

Allen is a very focused travel expert ensuring that his clients have stress free travel, total piece of mind and support 24 hours a day, 7 days a week.

Allen has been in the travel industry for more than 40 years and helps time-pressed travellers and corporations to manage their travel arrangements wherever they may be. Though Allen loves the internet, he is a great believer in travellers can make their own simple bookings, they must realise that in times of trouble, they are on their own with their travel arrangements, and a good travel agent is vital. His website is www.theonlytravelagent.com.

You can contact Allen on 1300 648 357 or email him at allens@travelmanagers.com.au

Liz O'Dwyer

Liz O'Dwyer is a customer experience professional. She assists SME's and solo-preneurs Australia wide to attract and retain customers, therefore achieving their business goals. As she works with business owners, she also by default assists them to achieve their personal goals as well. She will teach you ways to be able to differentiate your business from your competitor's through customer service excellence. This breeds new business for free.

To learn how to wow your customers, and grow a wildly successful business visit www.customercentricity.com.au today, or contact Liz on info@customercentricity.com.au.

Michelle Hext

Michelle Hext is CEO & founder of Glow Women's Fitness Online. Michelle's experience in business and the fitness industry is as varied as it is long, having been involved in owning and operating four gymnasiums, a personal training studio and 5 taekwondo schools over the last 19 years.

Michelle also developed Powerkick, a martial arts to music program developed for Martial Art's school owners so they could increase their schools income by introducing this popular type of program to their schools safely.

Michelle has written for Jetstars in flight magazine, Oxygen Magazine, Women's Fitness & Health, Body & Soul, Notebook and many more and was featured as one of Australia's Trainers to watch in 2010 in Ultrafit Magazine. You can contact Michelle at www.glowwomensfitnessonline.com.au or by email at michelle@glowwomensfitnessonline.com.au

Angela den Hollander

Angela den Hollander is the small biz, branding wiz and head honcho of communic8 design, a company that it is passionate about delivering big business branding strategies to small business owners.
She has worked in the advertising, design and marketing industries since the tender age of 16, starting in the finished art studio of a major advertising agency in Adelaide as a pesky work experience kid who just wouldn't leave.
Whether you're just starting out or have been running your business for many years, if you're struggling with defining what's unique about your business, and how to convey that to your potential clients, Angela can help. You can visit Angela at www.communic8design.com.au

Danielle Storey

Danielle and David Storey own The Cartridge Family. After an 11 year journey from poverty to success, The Cartridge Family is now a multi-million dollar Australian success stor(e)y that everyone wants to hear about. And Danielle and David are still happily married! With clearly defined roles, and a culture of fun in the office, The Cartridge Family management team and wonderful staff are delighting customers throughout Australia and New Zealand.
You can contact Danielle and other members of The Cartridge Family at **1300 1 TONER (1300 186 637)**

Dr Karina Butera

Karina is a forty-something social and business entrepreneur who specialises in facilitating positive cultural change through personal and professional development programs. She has worked and studied in New Zealand, Australia and the USA, with a business background spanning recruitment, sales and management consulting and an academic background in human and social behaviour. Karina's love of written expression and passion for 'ordinary people having a say' has seen her work read by a diverse audience - with publications in academic journals, newspapers, magazines, websites and learning/development materials.
Karina Butera, is the visionary and the founder of **High Ideals** "for those who put their actions where their values are"
Karina can be contacted at High Ideals www.high-ideals.com, by phone on 1300 313 205 or by email on karina.butera@high-ideals.com

Tania Smith

From the age of 12, Tania Smith knew she wanted to be an "enter-pre-newer". Although she couldn't pronounce the word properly, it sounded exciting!
Twenty three years later it happened, she became an entrepreneur who is passionate about business.
From shaky beginnings as a Virtual Assistant, not sure where the next client was coming from, to having a waiting list for Graphic and Web Design, her two businesses continue to go from strength to strength.
With her business partner (and husband) Scott, and their two young children Toby and Imogen, Tania enjoys offering her services to the world from her office in country Victoria, while overlooking the paddocks where sheep graze.
You can contact Tania by phone on: 1300 409 441 or via the web on www.backstagehelper.com

John McCann

John McCann is an Organisational and Performance Psychologist, an Executive coach, a Real Estate Coach and Mentor, a leadership consultant, and an author. He currently coaches high performing agents and principals Australia wide. He has a degree in Marketing and a Masters in Psychology, is a member of the Australian Psychological Society and is a Fellow of the Australian Institute of Management.
Prior to real estate John worked in large companies in Australia and North America.
John's real estate professional development practice www.orgpsych.com.au is based on his practical experience as an agent and the work of world renowned psychologists and researchers.
He has established a national network of accredited high performing ethical agents www.helperagent.com.au.

William McPherson

Bill (William) McPherson was the operator of a successful; plumbing business from 1950 which gave him the ability to diversify into other interests such as Importing, the Stock Market, a Winery, property, and several successful restaurants, all of which taught him the value of management and human relations.
Being a strong supporter of the Mens Shed Movement in Australia he is part of a team currently developing the Hobsons Bay Mens Shed at the Hobsons Bay Community Workshop which promises to be one of the most developed and diversified Sheds in Australia.
His current major interest is in printing and publishing community newspapers which can be seen at
www.aroundaltona.com.au and
www.aroundpointcook.com.au

Doreen Schwegler

Doreen Schwegler has been a Naturopath for over 20 years. She originally gained a Bachelors degree at RMIT University (Haematology major). After extensive travel and work in laboratories in Melbourne and overseas, she studied Naturopathy (SSNT) and now specialises in helping couples struggling with fertility issues, recurrent miscarriages, IVF, and those wanting to heave a healthy baby. She also does Bowen Therapy, and successful weight loss programs. Her Essendon clinic is a one-stop wellness centre with a team of fantastic health professionals including an Acupuncturist, Osteopath, Psychologist, Shiatsu and Massage Therapist. Yoga and Personal Training is also available.
You can contact Doreen at:
www.alldegreesofhealth.com.au or phone (03)93310951

Become a Published Author

We hope you have enjoyed this collection of SMART Business Builders.

If these stories have inspired you to want to share your story, or if you have been thinking about writing and publishing a book for a while and are just sitting on the brink then we can assist.

We are in the process of compiling additional books in the **"Smart People - Smart Business"** series, so if you have a story to tell why not share it with us and you never know it could be included in our next edition.

We can also assist you with publishing your own complete book if that would suit you better, you will be amazed at just how little it costs to get started.

As an example for as little as $250 you could have your very own book printed, published and ready for sale, you even get the opportunity to purchase your own books at wholesale for resale.

If you would like to know more just visit
www.smartpeoplesmartbusiness.com
and complete the on-line enquiry form.

Book cover designed by typengraphics
Helping Small Business Get Noticed by Design
Specialising in Graphic Design & Printing
PO Box 239 St Arnaud VIC 3478. Ph: 1300 409 441.

www.ingramcontent.com/pod-product-compliance
Lightning Source LLC
Chambersburg PA
CBHW051530170526
45165CB00002B/677